COMBAT LEGEND

SPITFIRE
Mks I–V

Peter R. Caygill

Airlife

Copyright © 2002 Airlife Publishing Ltd

Text written by Peter R. Caygill
Profile illustrations drawn by Dave Windle
Cover painting by Jim Brown – The Art of Aviation Co. Ltd

First published in the UK in 2002
by Airlife Publishing Ltd

British Library Cataloguing-in-Publication Data
  A catalogue record for this book
  is available from the British Library

ISBN 1 84037 391 1

Printed in China

*Contact us for a free catalogue that describes the complete range of Airlife
books for aviation enthusiasts.*
Airlife Publishing Ltd
101 Longden Road, Shrewsbury, SY3 9EB, England
E-mail: sales@airlifebooks.com
Website: www.airlifebooks.com

Contents

Spitfire Mks I–V Timeline

3 January 1935
Specification F.37/34 is issued by the Air Ministry to cover the Supermarine Type 300 fighter.

5 March 1936
Captain J. 'Mutt' Summers takes the prototype F.37/34 fighter, K5054, on its first flight from Eastleigh.

11 June 1937
Reginald J. Mitchell dies. Development of the Spitfire is taken over by Joe Smith.

14 May 1938
First production Spitfire Mk I (K9787) is flown by Jeffrey Quill from Eastleigh.

4 August 1938
No. 19 Squadron at Duxford receives its first Spitfire Mk I (K9789).

16 October 1939
Spitfire Mk Is of Nos 602 and 603 Squadrons shoot down two Junkers Ju 88s of KG 30 attempting to attack warships in the Firth of Forth.

18 November 1939
Flight Lieutenant M.V. Longbottom flies the first photo-reconnaissance sortie in a Spitfire PR.Mk IB from Seclin near Lille.

13 January 1940
Pilot Officer George Proudman of No. 72 Squadron becomes the first RAF pilot to shoot down an enemy bomber (a Heinkel He 111), while flying a Spitfire Mk IB (L1007) armed with 20-mm Hispano cannon.

16 March 1940
Jeffrey Quill completes the first flight of the Spitfire Mk III (N3297).

27 June 1940
Castle Bromwich factory delivers its first Spitfire (Mk II P7280).

26 September 1940
Supermarine's Woolston and Itchen factories are destroyed in a *Luftwaffe* raid.

February/March 1941
No. 92 Squadron at Biggin Hill is the first unit to convert to the Spitfire Mk V.

7 March 1942
The first Spitfire Mk VCs for Malta are flown from the deck of HMS *Eagle* during Operation *Spotter*.

2 June 1942
Six out of twelve Spitfire Mk VBs of No. 403 Squadron are shot down in an encounter with Focke-Wulf Fw 190s of JG 26.

19 August 1942
Some 42 squadrons of Spitfire Mk Vs provide air cover during Operation *Jubilee*, the Dieppe Raid.

June 1943
Spitfire LF.Mk VBs, fitted with 'cropped blower' Rolls-Royce Merlin 45Ms, become operational.

6 June 1944
Supermarine Spitfire LF.Mk VB fighter-bombers of No. 611 Squadron are the first RAF fighters to mount patrol over the Normandy landings on D-Day.

1. Prototypes and Development

Although Reginald Mitchell was to design what is arguably the most beautiful aircraft ever built, not all of his creations pleased the eye. Following his graceful Schneider racers, his next single-engined monoplane, the Supermarine Type 224, which was the immediate predecessor of the Spitfire, had little in the way of elegance. It featured a thick-section, inverted gull-wing of long span, which gave the impression that strength considerations had been the primary design aim rather than aerodynamic efficiency. There is an element of truth in this as Mitchell's S.4 seaplane had crashed as a result of wing flutter. However, the Type 224's form was dictated to a large extent by the use of a 660-hp Rolls-Royce Goshawk engine that employed evaporative cooling.

Forerunner of the Spitfire, the Supermarine Type 224, K2890, is seen at Eastleigh in the summer of 1934. It is wearing its participation number for the Hendon Air Pageant, which was held that year on 30 June. *(Philip Jarrett)*

The Supermarine Type 224, having been modified with a large wing root fillet at the trailing edge and fitted with wool tufts to ascertain airflow characteristics. This formed part of the design evolution that resulted in the Spitfire, and was done to eradicate tail buffet. *(Philip Jarrett)*

The aim of this form of engine cooling was to avoid the drag penalty of conventional radiators. It was eventually found to be impracticable in low-wing monoplanes, although only after much time and effort had been expended in trying to make the system work. The coolant water was pressurised to prevent it from boiling and on leaving the engine it was then depressurised, the resultant steam being fed to a condenser situated in the leading edge of the wing. As the steam turned back into water it was then returned to the system via collector tanks in the fixed undercarriage fairings. The main problem concerned pumping the water back up to the header tank, as the necessary reduction in

pressure often caused the coolant to revert to steam once again, which led to the pump ceasing to function.

Along with seven other designs, the Type 224 was produced to Specification F.7/30, but its performance was disappointing with a top speed of only 238 mph and a time to 15,000 ft of 8 minutes. The competition was eventually won by the Gloster SS.37, which was developed into the Gladiator. While the troubled Type 224 was still being tested, Mitchell came up with a revised design (Type 300) featuring retractable undercarriage and shortened span. It was hoped that the top speed could be raised to around 265 mph but the Air Ministry's response was less than ecstatic and Mitchell was forced to further refine his proposals. Another 3 ft came off the wing (it was also made thinner) and the speed was now estimated at 280 mph.

A new Rolls-Royce engine

In late 1934 the new Rolls-Royce PV.12 was offered. It was already producing 625 hp for take-off, with the prospect of much more to come. Mitchell incorporated this new powerplant into his design but as it weighed 30 per cent more than the Goshawk, the wing of the Type 300 had to be altered, the eventual result being the now familiar elliptical planform. This produced several benefits, the relatively wide chord at the root eased structural considerations and allowed space for the undercarriage, while at the same time keeping thickness to chord ratio low. Another advantage was that the narrow, pointed wing tips were

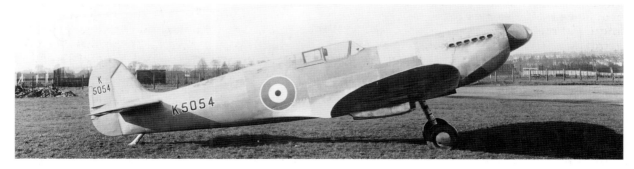

Photographed at Eastleigh shortly before its first flight on 5 March 1936, the prototype F.37/34, K5054, shows the original horn balance for the rudder and lack of undercarriage doors (the gear was locked down for the maiden flight). Other notable features are the tailskid, flat-topped canopy and short stub exhausts. *(Philip Jarrett)*

K5054 being flown by 'Mutt' Summers on 11 May 1936. By this time the prototype had been painted in a high-gloss light blue/grey colour scheme, the rudder horn balance had been reduced in size and the top of the fin revised. *(Philip Jarrett)*

ideally shaped to keep induced drag to a minimum. The revised Type 300 was offered to the Air Ministry and the contract for a prototype was issued on 1 December 1934, to be followed by a specification (F.37/34) on 3 January 1935.

At this stage evaporative cooling was still a requirement and the Type 300 was to have had a retractable ventral radiator for use during take-off and in the climb with the main cooling system taking over once the aircraft was at its operational height. Continuing problems with evaporative cooling on the Type 224 led to the concept being abandoned during 1935, thus forcing Mitchell to use conventional fixed radiators. As speed was one of the prime requirements of the new fighter, the use of drag-inducing radiators may have been seen as a retrograde step although developments in two fields led to the deficiencies of a fixed installation being kept to a minimum. The use of ethylene glycol, with its higher boiling point, allowed the radiator to be built smaller. In addition, work at the Royal Aircraft Establishment (RAE) at Farnborough by Dr Frederick Meredith reduced the negative aspects still further. He proposed mounting the radiator in a duct of varying width, one that was divergent upstream of the radiator, thereby decreasing velocity and increasing pressure. After the air had gone through the radiator and been heated, it then passed through the remainder of the duct, which was convergent, resulting in the air being ejected at increased velocity. The resultant thrust went some way towards offsetting the drag created.

Another significant development was the change to eight guns in place of four as specified in F.37/34. Due to the increased speed of the proposed new fighters (the prototype Hawker Hurricane was already being built) it was felt that less time would be available to achieve a decisive result in air combat and that a heavier weight of fire was needed. One of the main proponents of this theory was Squadron Leader Ralph Sorley of the Operational Requirements branch of the Air Ministry, whose ideas became widely held, so much so that they were incorporated into specifications F.5/34 and F.10/35. The latter requested six (but preferably eight) guns, which Mitchell was able to accommodate in the wings of his new fighter. F.10/35 also called for a reduced fuel capacity of 66 Imp gal (as opposed to 94 Imp gal in F.37/34)

7

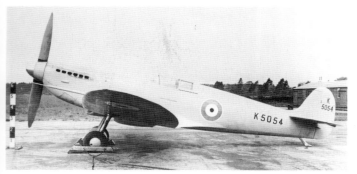

In this view of K5054, undercarriage doors have been incorporated and a long pitot tube has been fitted to the port wing for trials by the A&AEE at Martlesham Heath. Note also the two-bladed, fixed-pitch wooden propeller. *(Philip Jarrett)*

although the prototype was to emerge with a capacity of 75 Imp gal. One of the last major changes to the design of the Type 300 was the raising of its tailplane by 7 in, to alleviate problems with spin recovery that had been brought to light during trials with a 1:24th scale model in the wind tunnel at Farnborough.

Maiden flight

By early 1936 construction of the new Supermarine fighter (K5054) was virtually complete and it was flown for the first time by Vickers Chief Test Pilot Captain J. 'Mutt' Summers from Eastleigh on 5 March. The PV.12 engine was now known as the Merlin, the 'C' Type as fitted to K5054 producing 990 hp. A few weeks later the name Spitfire was proposed, a name that had also been used unofficially in relation to the Type 224. Initial flight trials were encouraging. The rudder horn balance had to be reduced to eradicate some directional instability and although top speed was below expectations, it was hoped the use of more advanced propellers would allow 350 mph to be achieved. Eventually it was concluded that the tips of the two-bladed, fixed-pitch propeller might be suffering from excessive drag rise due to compressibility, and when the profile was modified a speed of 348 mph was recorded, sufficient to give the Spitfire a clear advantage over the Hurricane. This was highly significant for Supermarine, since the Hurricane's speed had previously been within 5 mph of the Spitfire's speed and it was imperative for the latter to find more speed for its production status to be ensured. Although the first Spitfire was limited to a maximum Indicated Airspeed (IAS) of 380 mph to prevent any possibility of wing flutter, production aircraft had a strengthened wing and were cleared up to 470 mph IAS.

The prototype Spitfire continued to fly until 4 September 1939 when it was involved in a fatal accident on landing at Farnborough, killing its pilot, Flight Lieutenant G.S White. Prior to this it was involved in a number of trials including the

K5054 pictured after a forced landing on 22 March 1937. It had been flying from Martlesham Heath to test alterations to the elevator control system when Flying Officer Sam McKenna experienced engine failure. By this time the aircraft had been fitted with eight 0.303-in Browning machine-guns in the wings and streamlined exhaust manifolds. *(Philip Jarrett)*

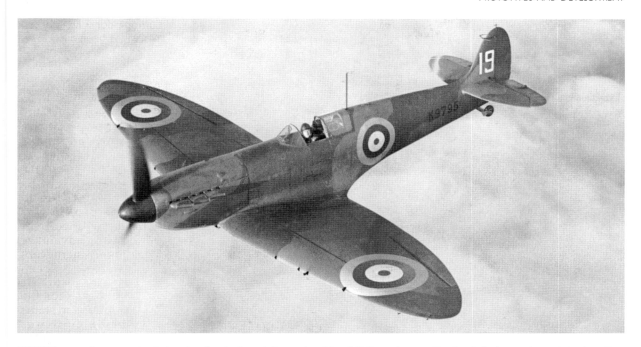

K9795 was photographed shortly after being delivered to No. 19 Squadron at Duxford. It shows the original radio mast, flat-topped hood and horn balance guard for an anti-spin parachute. It went on to fly with Nos 64, 603 and 222 Squadrons, before being used by No. 58 Operational Training Unit (OTU). *(Philip Jarrett)*

fitting of two different types of tailwheel, one featuring a single Dunlop wheel and the other a twin-wheeled arrangement that was quickly discarded as it was prone to seizure due to mud accumulation. During its early development the first Spitfire achieved extra performance, thanks to the efforts of Ray Dorey and Harry Pearson at Rolls-Royce. They came up with the ejector exhaust system that utilised the propulsive thrust of the engine exhaust to increase top speed by around 10 mph. K5054 was also used to test a system of gun heating (the standard armament of eight Browning 0.303-in machine-guns having been fitted in late 1936). Trials had shown that at altitudes of around 30,000 ft the guns were prone to stoppage (if they worked at all) and it was not until October 1938 that the difficulties were largely overcome by ducting hot air from the radiator (later, Spitfire Mk Vs were fitted with exhaust intensifier tubes to augment the hot air taken from the radiator).

By this time the first production Spitfires had flown and No. 19 Squadron was beginning its work-up period at Duxford. The structure of the new fighter was radical and featured extensive use of stressed skin construction. The fuselage was built in three sections, the main part extending from the forward fireproof bulkhead to the tail section. This was built up from four main longerons and fifteen transverse frames, those behind the cockpit were oval in section, with the forward five being of 'U' section to accommodate fuel tanks and the cockpit area. The structure was further stiffened by longitudinal 'Z'-section intercostals. Forward of the bulkhead was a tubular engine mounting and the tail unit (which was also a metal monocoque) was attached to the fuselage by a series of bolts and studs.

Advanced wing design
One of the most advanced features of the Spitfire was the design of its wing. Structural loads were taken by a single spar consisting of two square-section booms with a plate web which formed a strong 'D'-shaped torsion box with the heavy-duty leading edge skinning. A secondary spar carried the split flaps and fabric-covered

ailerons. The wings were attached to the fuselage by three bolts at the mainspar fixing position (adjacent to the fireproof bulkhead) and a single bolt at the auxiliary spar (frame 10). The immensely strong forward section of the wing gave good resistance to flutter and also allowed the wing to be built much thinner, which improved high speed handling. Although the term critical Mach number had not yet been coined, the Spitfire's characteristics at high Mach were superior to any of its contemporaries and were even better than most early jet fighters.

The first Spitfires flew with a number of different propellers, beginning with the prototype's wooden two-bladed fixed-pitch de Havilland airscrew. K5054 was later tested with a two-position, three-bladed de Havilland metal propeller but as general performance at operational heights showed little improvement, early production Spitfires were delivered with wooden two-bladed Weybridge airscrews. The three-blader had, however, given better figures for take-off and in the climb, and eventually it was realised that these were advantages well worth having. The three-bladed de Havilland propeller was fitted from the 78th production

Spitfire Mk Is of No. 19 Squadron lined up for the press at Duxford on 4 May 1939. By now, some aircraft have domed hoods fitted and all have had the squadron's 'WZ' codes applied. As yet there is no evidence of the 'bulletproof' glass panel to the windscreen, armour behind the pilot's seat, or gyro gunsight. *(Philip Jarrett)*

Before and after: Two views of K9912 'YT-O' of No. 65 Squadron. The photograph above shows the aircraft in its prime at Hornchurch in June 1939. At right the aircraft is seen after Pilot Officer K.G. Hart had carried out a forced landed on the beach near Dunkirk on 26 May 1940, having lost out in an encounter with a Bf 109E. Hart then set fire to the aircraft and returned home by boat. (Both Philip Jarrett)

aircraft, and when coupled to a Merlin III (first fitted to the 175th Spitfire Mk I), improved top speed by 5 mph to 367 mph. The Merlin III was also capable of accepting a three-bladed metal Rotol airscrew. By the time of the Battle of Britain, a programme had been set in motion to change all two-position units with Rotol or de Havilland constant speed propellers that automatically adjusted blade pitch for each condition of flight.

Prior to the outbreak of war a domed hood was introduced to increase headroom, and protection was later added for the pilot with a bulletproof panel of 1.75-in thickness on the outside of the windscreen and 0.25-in armour plating behind the headrest. Consideration had also been given to improving the Spitfire's armament by replacing four of its Browning guns with two 20-mm Hispano cannon. These weapons were required since bombers were beginning to appear with armour protection and self-sealing fuel tanks, so that even eight rifle-calibre machine-guns might not have sufficient weight of fire to destroy a target in a short burst. The first 20-mm Hispano guns were fitted to

L1007 in June 1939 and the first of the problems associated with the installation became evident with frequent stoppages. Use of the Hispano led to the eight-gun Spitfire being referred to as the Mk IA ('A' Type wing) with the cannon version as the IB ('B' Type wing).

Spitfire Mk II

The first of many new versions of the Spitfire appeared in June 1940 with the delivery of the first Spitfire Mk II. The Mk II was built only at Castle Bromwich and featured a 1,175-hp Merlin XII that was fired up by a Coffman starter cartridge. The Spitfire Mk II was virtually indistinguishable from the Mk I, except for a small teardrop-shaped blister on the starboard cowling immediately behind the spinner that covered part of the gearing for the starter. The first Spitfire Mk IIs were delivered to No. 611 Squadron in August 1940 and eventually a total of 920 was built, of which 750 were Mk IIAs, the rest being cannon-armed Mk IIBs.

A more radical revision of the basic Spitfire design resulted in the Mk III, although in the event only one definitive example (N3297) was produced. It was flown for the first time on 16 March 1940, its appearance showing that there had been considerable attention to detail in an attempt to improve performance. The tailwheel was retractable and small flaps attached to the mainwheel fairings covered the portion of the tyre that had previously remained exposed when retracted. There was also a much neater windscreen design, with the bulletproof glazing mounted internally rather than externally, and the wing span was reduced to 32 ft 7 in (from 36 ft 10 in). The wings were also of revised construction to allow for various combinations of guns, either eight 0.303-in Brownings, two 20-mm Hispano cannon and four Brownings, or four Hispano cannon. The Mk III had a two-speed supercharged Merlin XX of 1,240 hp, the extra power requiring strengthening of the forward fuselage and engine mountings. Other modifications included a general beefing up of the undercarriage legs, which were also angled forward by a further two inches in an attempt to avoid the Spitfire's tendency to nose-over in soft-field conditions.

The Spitfire Mk III offered a top speed of around 385 mph, but was in trouble almost from the start. Development difficulties with the Merlin XX led to delays and the decision was then taken to award priority of engine supply to the Hurricane Mk II, which would have quickly become obsolescent without it. Supermarine also underestimated the amount of time it would take to organise deliveries of the re-engineered

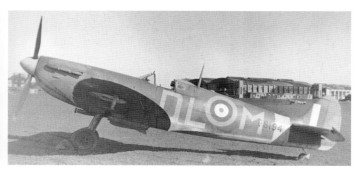

Spitfire Mk IIA P8194 'DL-M', of No. 91 Squadron, later flew with Nos 234, 66 and 152 Squadrons, as well as No. 57 OTU. It was also used by de Havilland for trials with a 'reverse thrust' propeller that could operate at a negative angle of attack after touch-down to reduce the landing run. *(Philip Jarrett)*

fighter, but it was clear that the RAF could not entertain any shortfall in production. Another factor was the possibility that the Battle of Britain would have to be fought all over again in 1941. If this happened it was likely that the air battles of the future would take place at higher altitudes than had been the case in 1940. The *Luftwaffe* had recently introduced the Messerschmitt Bf 109F, which was capable of operating at heights in excess of 30,000 ft and Junkers Ju 86P reconnaissance aircraft had also been seen flying over the UK at heights estimated to be around 40,000 ft. It was clear that performance at high altitude would be one of the prime requirements in future fighter aircraft.

Spitfire Mk V

One of the main production difficulties with the Merlin XX concerned its low-altitude blower, but ironically, the RAF's operational requirement was now heavily weighted towards performance at higher altitudes. In parallel with the Merlin XX, Rolls-Royce had been developing a similar version which featured a single blower of 10.25-in diameter. Known as the Merlin 45, it gave a power output of 1,440 hp and promised to make the Spitfire much more effective at greater heights. As it could also be easily adapted to the Mk I/II airframe with the minimum amount of modification, the Spitfire Mk III was effectively killed off. Therefore, on 6 March 1941, Air Chief Marshal Sir Charles Portal gave the go-ahead for the Spitfire Mk V to be put into quantity production. Following the rejection of the Spitfire Mk III, N3297 was fitted with standard wings and was used by Rolls-Royce at Hucknall to test the new RM6SM engine which was developed into the Merlin 61 of the Spitfire Mk IX. The Spitfire Mk V was to be built in greater numbers than any other Spitfire variant, but was initially considered to be only a temporary stop-gap until the Mk VI came along, with its pressure cabin and extended wing tips (the Mk IV was the first of the Griffon Spitfires and is discussed later). In appearance the Spitfire Mk V was virtually identical to those that had gone before, its main recognition feature being a revised oil cooler under the port wing which was of circular cross section, instead of semi-circular. There was also a slightly altered nose profile and the tubular engine mounting forward of the bulkhead was strengthened to cater for the heavier Merlin 45. The engine itself featured revisions to the supercharger impeller and diffuser which improved overall efficiency by around 10 per cent. The air intake ducting was also completely revised so that pressure losses were minimised. Take-off boost on the

Right: Spitfire Mk III N3297 displays clipped wings, small wheel doors similar to those used on K5054, redesigned windscreen and retractable tailwheel. It was powered by a Rolls-Royce Merlin XX, but despite having a significantly improved performance, did not go into production. *(Philip Jarrett)*

R6923 first flew on 12 July 1940 and was fitted with a 'B' Type wing prior to joining No. 19 Squadron later that month. Following the withdrawal of cannon-armed aircraft, it flew with No. 7 OTU before being delivered to No. 92 Squadron and was flown by Pilot Officer Allan Wright to Hucknall on 7 April 1941, to be converted to Mk VB standard by Rolls-Royce. R6923 failed to return from an escort sortie on 21 June 1941. Sergeant G.W. Aston baled out successfully and was rescued; however, five days later he did the same thing in P8532 and was taken PoW. *(Philip Jarrett)*

In a long career, W3822 *Zanzibar IV* survived stalling on take-off from Martlesham Heath on 14 October 1941 with No. 403 Squadron, before going on to serve with Nos 129, 602, 66, 234 and 312 Squadrons. It was Struck off Charge (SOC) on 27 June 1946. *(Philip Jarrett)*

Merlin 45 was raised to +12 lb/sq in, with maximum combat boost of +16 lb/sq in limited to 5 minutes' duration.

Initially two versions of the Mk V were produced, the Mk VA with eight 0.303-in Brownings and the Mk VB with two 20-mm Hispano cannon and four Brownings. These were followed by the Mk VC, which possessed a strengthened wing employing much of the development that had gone into the wing of the Mk III. Known as the Type 'C' or 'universal' wing, it could accommodate either of the armament options of the earlier versions, or four 20-mm Hispano cannon. The first Spitfire Mk Vs were in fact converted Mk IBs, No. 92 Squadron sending its old aircraft to Hucknall in batches of two or three, for the new engine to be fitted and other modifications carried out. This process took about a week and by the end of March 1941 most of the squadron's aircraft had been brought up to Mk V standard.

The Spitfire Mk V saw service in most theatres of World War Two and was the means by which Fighter Command took the fight to the German forces in occupied France. It also went on far longer than anyone at the time could have envisaged, and was modified over the course of time to suit local conditions and maintain its effectiveness in the air. The Spitfire Mk V was the first variant to see service in the Mediterranean when fifteen Mk VBs were flown off the deck of HMS *Eagle* on 7 March 1942 to reinforce the island of Malta. These, and subsequent aircraft, were 'tropicalised' by the fitting of a Vokes filter for the carburettor intake in a large chin-type fairing under the nose. Due to a reduction in ram air pressure, and the drag caused by the fairing, top speed was reduced by about 8 mph and the climb rate was also lower. Later, a much smaller filter was devised by No. 103 MU at Aboukir, which reduced performance loss and was fitted to many Spitfire Mk Vs in the Middle East.

Since the Spitfire had been designed as a short-range defensive fighter, its meagre 85-Imp gal internal fuel capacity was inadequate for the offensive work it was later asked to do. The Mk V therefore introduced the type's first successful overload fuel tank. This was of streamlined shape and fitted under the centre section. Of either 30- or 45-Imp gal capacity, the tank was jettisoned before entering combat and allowed increased range, or the use of higher power settings to maintain high speed when enemy fighters were likely to be encountered. To jettison the tank the cock control had to be moved to the OFF position and the jettison lever pulled up, both controls being situated on the right-hand side of the cockpit. Larger tanks of 90- and 170-Imp gal were used for ferry purposes, the latter allowing Spitfires to fly to Malta direct from Gibraltar. The degree of manoeuvre was strictly limited, however, and aircraft fitted with the 170-Imp gal tank were only cleared to fly straight and level.

Low-altitude specialists

The most far-reaching modifications to affect the Spitfire Mk V were to change its operational role. The emergence of the Fw 190A in the summer of 1941, with its superior performance, put great pressure on RAF Fighter Command and in the short term there was little that it could do to counter the new machine. The ultimate salvation would come with the Spitfire Mk IX, with its two-stage, two-speed Merlin 61, but with the Mk IX unlikely to be in widespread use before mid-1943 and the Mk V in mass production, the fighter situation in the short term was extremely serious. It was the engineers at Rolls-Royce that came up with a solution, with the so-called M-series Merlin. This featured a cropped supercharger impeller that allowed full power to be delivered at a lower height and also increased maximum combat boost to +18 lb/sq in. Use of this engine brought the Mk V's performance into line with that of the Fw 190A, but only at low to medium levels, as speed and acceleration began to fall off dramatically at heights above 12,000 ft.

Spitfire Mk Vs fitted with the M-series Merlin 45/50/55 were re-designated LF.Mk V, the LF

AA878 was another presentation Spitfire and carried the title *Manchester Merchant Trader*. The first production Mk VC, it was retained for armament trials and is seen here with four 20-mm Hispano cannon. It subsequently flew with Nos 411, 341 and 453 Squadrons, before suffering a landing mishap at Sumburgh. Repairs were carried out by London, Midland and Scottish Railway (LMS) and AA878 was delivered to No. 1 Tactical Exercise Unit (TEU) on 17 August 1944. It was SOC on 25 October 1945. *(Philip Jarrett)*

denoting Low-Altitude Fighter. The first modified machines were introduced in the summer of 1943 and due to use of the new engine the Mk V's role was restricted to the close escort of medium bombers, low-level cover and ground attack. Many LF.Mk Vs also featured clipped wings, whereby the detachable wing tips were removed and replaced by a streamlined fairing. This feature had first been seen on the Spitfire Mk III, its chief advantage being that rate of roll was improved, one facet of performance in which the Fw 190 was particularly good. There was also a slight increase in top speed at low level, but turn radius was increased and stall speed went up marginally. Although there were clear benefits, many pilots chose to retain the wing tips and some squadrons flew a mix of clipped and unclipped aircraft. Pilots invariably referred to the LF.Mk V as the 'clipped, cropped and clapped' Spitfire, although there appear to be two schools of thought regarding the term 'clapped'. For many it relates to the aircraft's age, as all Spitfire LFs were second-hand, but there are still those who maintain that the appellation refers to its lack of performance at altitude.

Testing the Mk V

Prior to flying Spitfire HF.Mk VIIs and the first Gloster Meteor jet fighters with No. 616 Squadron, Flight Lieutenant Clive

Spitfire Mk VB (trop) AB344 was flown for the first time on 17 January 1942 and was dispatched to Gibraltar for transfer to the aircraft carrier HMS *Eagle*. It was one of the first 15 Spitfires to fly to Malta on 7 March 1942 (Operation *Spotter*), but was destroyed on the ground at Kalafrana on 18 April. Total flying time amounted to 14 hours 20 minutes. *(Philip Jarrett)*

Gosling was a production test pilot and recalls the time he spent testing the Spitfire Mk V at Supermarine: 'The Mk V to me seemed underpowered, indeed it was not until the airframe was fitted with the Merlin 61 that its full potential appeared to be realised. Initially in the V there were problems with longitudinal stability which was caused by the loading instructions being ignored at MUs and in the squadrons, and resulted in a number of aircraft breaking up in the air as they [the pilots] over-controlled on applying *g*. Although the aircraft were lively as the cg [centre of gravity] was well aft, they could be dangerous. The instability was dealt with by putting a 6.5-lb weight on an arm in the elevator circuit – the effect of this was as *g* was applied, the weight pulled the control column forward, so preventing over-control. This was not popular on the squadrons, where pilots complained of a loss of manoeuvrability as they had to pull harder on the control column in tight turns and that the control jerked to and fro when taxying, but it did stop people being killed.

'The other deficiency of the early marks was that the ailerons became virtually immovable at high speeds. This was due to the distortion of the fabric cover and it was not until metal ailerons were introduced that a great improvement was made. The V just about matched the 109F in performance but when the Fw 190 came along it was outclassed. We had trouble with the tropicalised Spitfires to begin with, as in a dive the air intake would collapse. This caused a lot of worry as the aircraft carrier was waiting in Glasgow to load them for Malta. The intake was strengthened very quickly and they caught the boat. Much later the very neat intake designed in the Middle East [Aboukir filter] encouraged Supermarine to do their own. During the first overload tank trials petrol was finding its way into the fuselage which was disconcerting, especially as I was doing the trials! It was cured by making small modifications to the aerodynamics of the tank.

'The LF.Mk V was a little 'hot rod', very nimble and light, it was exhilarating to fly and at low level you would see 340–350 mph on the ASI. Its rate of climb was also very good. I flew the Mark XII prototype (DP845) against Jeffrey Quill flying an LF.V and at full power we reached 15,000 ft together. However, due to the greater power of

The first Griffon-engined Spitfire, DP845, is seen here with a mock-up installation of six 20-mm Hispano cannon. It later became the Spitfire Mk XX, before becoming the prototype Spitfire Mk XII. *(Philip Jarrett)*

the Griffon I was able to gain on JKQ in a turn and when he rolled under and dived away I was able to catch him easily in the dive.'

In its later life the Spitfire Mk V was modified to carry a bomb of up to 500 lb on a standard bomb carrier fitted to an adaptor attached to the fuselage centre section. With its strengthened wing, the VC was able to carry a 250-lb bomb under each wing. The bomb release button was mounted on the throttle control lever on the left-hand side of the cockpit.

Spitfire Mk IV

Although it preceded the Mk V in number sequence, Mk IV was the designation initially given to the first Spitfire to be powered by a Rolls-Royce Griffon engine. The aircraft did not fly until 27 November 1941. At 27-litre capacity, the Merlin was a relatively small engine, in comparison the Daimler-Benz DB 601N that powered the Bf 109F was 33.9 litres and the 14-cylinder BMW 801D-2 radial in the Fw 190A had a capacity of 41.8 litres. With the Merlin, Rolls-Royce had chosen to utilise its expertise in the field of supercharging to a high degree, but even though the engine was capable of

considerable development, it was clear that a larger unit would be needed before long. In fact, one already existed as the 36.7-litre Griffon was based on the Type R engine used in the Schneider racers and had been bench-run as long ago as 1932. In developed form it promised much, and Rolls-Royce worked wonders in keeping its frontal area and length within the necessary parameters so that it could be considered as an engine for advanced versions of the Spitfire. As the Griffon weighed 600 lb more than the Merlin, the fuselage structure of the Spitfire had to be strengthened and steel longerons were used in place of the original dural sections.

The prototype Spitfire Mk IV (DP845) had a lengthened fuselage 30 ft 6 in long, standard wings and a retractable tailwheel as used on the Mk III. The Griffon IIB had a single-stage supercharger and drove a four-bladed propeller. Armament was as in previous marks, although it was proposed that the Griffon-powered Spitfire would have the option of carrying up to six 20-mm Hispano cannon, and DP845 was mocked-up for a time in this configuration. Sometime in early 1942, the Mk IV was re-designated as the Mk XX to avoid confusion with the latest photo-reconnaissance Spitfire, the PR.Mk IV. DP845 flew for a time as the Mk XX before becoming the prototype Spitfire Mk XII

(late-mark Spitfires are to be covered in a second volume in the Combat Legends series).

In addition to excelling as a fighter and fighter-bomber, the Spitfire was one of the first true reconnaissance aircraft in the modern sense, since it flew high and fast and used its speed to evade enemy defences. The first PR Spitfires (N3069 and N3071) were delivered to Sidney Cotton's Heston Flight in October 1939, and were standard Mk Is with their guns removed and two F.24 cameras with 5-in focal length lenses installed in the inboard gun positions. After careful filling of all cracks, the aircraft were painted in 'Camotint', a pale green colour devised by Cotton. Following a change of designation to No. 2 Camouflage Unit to disguise the unit's purpose, the first missions were carried out on 18 November, when Flying Officer Maurice Longbottom flew from Seclin near Lille to photograph Aachen. The first operation was not a resounding success, but further sorties proved that the Spitfire was well suited to the reconnaissance task.

The first photo-reconnaissance Spitfires were designated PR.Mk IA and these were joined in early 1940 by the PR.Mk IB, which had an additional fuel tank of 29 Imp gal fitted behind the pilot. 'Camotint' was quickly replaced by PRU Blue and there was a further unit designation change, to Photographic Development Unit (PDU), a detachment at Seclin becoming No. 212 Squadron. By July, the PDU had become a Photographic Reconnaissance Unit (PRU), by which time No. 212 Squadron had been absorbed back into the parent unit following the fall of France. In March 1940 the first PR.Mk ICs were delivered with fuel capacity now increased by 59 Imp gal. In addition to the fuselage tank as used on the PR.Mk IB, the PR.Mk IC had another 30 Imp gal in a blister under the port wing, with a similar (flattened) blister under the starboard wing housing two F.24 cameras of 8-in focal length. The extra range now allowed targets as far away as Kiel to be photographed by the Spitfires.

Next in line of the high-flying PR Spitfires was the PR.Mk IF, which carried 30 Imp gal of fuel in both underwing blisters as well as 29 Imp gal in the fuselage tank. The cameras were relocated to the fuselage aft of the cockpit, and comprised two F.24s with 8-in focal length lenses (later 20-in). For low-level oblique photography, the single example of the PR.Mk IE (N3117) was delivered in June 1940. It was equipped with an F.24 camera in a bulged fairing under each wing, and this was augmented by the PR.Mk IG which retained the normal eight-gun armament. Unlike the Type E (PR.Mk IE) it had the 29-Imp gal fuselage tank and had an F.24 camera mounted obliquely behind the cockpit and two vertically mounted F.24s.

The true long-range photo-reconnaissance Spitfire was the PR.Mk ID, which carried fuel in the leading edges of its wing, a position that had previously been reserved for the condenser units of the evaporative cooling system. A total of 57 Imp gal was carried in each wing in the first two machines, but this was increased to 66.5 Imp gal in production examples, which allowed the fuselage tank to be deleted. Other modifications included the fitting of a Merlin 45 in place of the Merlin III, the addition of cabin heating and the installation of a radio – this had previously been omitted to save weight. The Type D was manufactured in large numbers (229 in all) and it was subsequently designated PR.Mk IV. Similarly the PR.Mk IG became the PR.Mk VII. A development, the PR.Mk XIII, featured a 1,660-hp Merlin 32 driving a four-bladed Rotol propeller and was armed with four 0.303-in Browning machine-guns. Only 25 Spitfire PR.Mk XIIIs were produced, all being conversions of Mark Vs by Heston Aircraft.

2. Operational History

On 4 August 1938 the first Spitfire Mk I was delivered to No. 19 Squadron at Duxford. By the time war was declared, eight more squadrons had re-equipped (Nos 41, 54, 65, 66, 72, 74, 602 and 611) with two more in the process of conversion (Nos 603 and 609). The first of many victories occurred on 16 October 1939, when two Ju 88s of KG 30 were shot down over the North Sea by Spitfires of Nos 602 and 603 Squadrons. The first German aircraft to be brought down on British soil in World War Two was an He 111 that crashed near Dalkeith in Scotland, again as a result of action by Nos 602 and 603 Squadrons.

The first major action in which the Spitfire was involved was the cover operation for the Dunkirk evacuations from 26 May to 3 June 1940. As Fighter Command was a defensive force trained to operate over home territory, it was somewhat ironic that its first major task was to seek out the enemy on the other side of the Channel. Standing patrols were flown whenever possible to prevent

A line-up of No. 65 Squadron Spitfire Mk Is at Hornchurch on 8 June 1939. The aircraft are carrying pre-war 'FZ' codes but there is variety as regards undersurface colour. The second and third aircraft in line have black/white undersides, while the first and fourth do not. The placard on the first machine reads 'Serviceable – Aeroplane No. K9912'. *(Philip Jarrett)*

Spitfire Mk I P9450 was first flown by Supermarine test pilot George Pickering on 5 April 1940, before being issued to No. 64 Squadron at Kenley. It was lost on 5 December 1940, when it was shot down by a Bf 109E, possibly being flown by *Oberst* Adolf Galland, *Kommodore* of JG 26, over the Channel. P9450's pilot, Sergeant C.L. Hopgood, was killed. *(Philip Jarrett)*

German bombers from attacking the mass of shipping in the Channel, but even the Spitfire squadrons suffered serious losses. In all, 46 Spitfires were lost during the Dunkirk period, resulting in the death of 28 pilots with another four being taken as prisoners of war (PoWs). These figures include three squadron commanders and three flight commanders. The hardest hit unit was No. 610 Squadron, which lost eight aircraft and seven pilots including its CO, Squadron Leader A.L. Franks.

With the fall of France on 22 June it was only a matter of time before *Luftwaffe* attention was transferred to Britain, the first probing attacks on shipping in the Channel beginning in July, by which time Fighter Command possessed 16 squadrons of Spitfires. It is not proposed to retell the story of the Battle of Britain, rather to describe the first (and last) large-scale attack on the north-east of England, on 15 August, through the eyes of No. 41 Squadron, which was based at Catterick.

Following an uneventful early morning patrol by three Spitfires, the squadron was scrambled just after midday and ordered to patrol 10 miles north of base. With Squadron Leader H.R.L. Hood on leave, No. 41 (callsign MITRE) was to

have been led by Flight Lieutenant Norman Ryder, but radio failure shortly after take-off meant that he had to hand over lead to Pilot Officer George Bennions. Weather conditions were eight-tenths cloud between 3,500 and 5,000 ft, haze up to 12,000 ft, visibility 30 miles, but only 4 miles in the haze layer. Squadron composition was as follows:

Yellow section	1: P/O G.H. Bennions	2: F/L E.N. Ryder
	3: P/O O.B. M-Ryan	4: P/O R.J. Boret
Red section	1: P/O J.N. MacKenzie	2: Sgt R.C. Ford
	3: P/O E.S. Lock	
Blue section	1: P/O A.D.J. Lovell	2: Sgt I.E. Howitt
	3: P/O G.A. Langley	
Green section	1: P/O E.A. Shipman	2: P/O R.W. Wallens
	3: Sgt F. Usmar	

A large German formation was seen 20 minutes after take-off, by which time it was in the area of Seaham harbour to the south of Sunderland. It comprised approximately 50 He 111H-4s of I. and III./KG 26 in a mass arrowhead formation, escorted by an estimated 40 Messerschmitt Bf 110Ds of I./ZG 76, both formations having taken off from

Stavanger/Sola in Norway about two hours before. Bennions (R6604) dispatched Green and Blue sections to attack the 110s, while he led Yellow and Red sections towards the bombers, ordering a No. 1 fighter attack in line-astern formation. The escorts maintained their position, however, and he was forced to break off an attempted beam attack and dive underneath and around to the rear of the 110s. Bennions then fired a burst at the rearmost 110, the port engine of which immediately began to smoke, before attacking another with similar result. This aircraft fell away and went into cloud near Barnard Castle, trailing petrol vapour or glycol. It was the machine of *Oberleutnant* Hans-Ulrich Kettling and *Obergefreiter* Fritz Volk which crash-landed near the village of Streatlam, the crew being taken prisoner.

Flight Lieutenant Norman Ryder (P9428) attacked a 'Ju 88' causing a 'violent crimson explosion' in the centre of the fuselage before it descended into cloud. The other members of Yellow section, Pilot Officers O.B. Morrough-Ryan (P9430) and R.J. Boret (R6605), also

attacked two of the bombers but lost them in cloud, the former being credited with one damaged (in their combat reports a number of pilots claimed to have attacked Ju 88s – although aircraft of this type belonging to KG 30 raided Driffield airfield and Bridlington around the same time, none ventured into No. 41 Squadron's territory).

After the aborted beam attack, Pilot Officer J.N. MacKenzie (R6756) led Red section in a climbing turn to get above the enemy formation and singled out one of the bombers which had become detached. His attack was pressed home to 80 yards, the fire from his eight machine-guns causing the enemy aircraft to veer sharply to the right as its starboard motor lost power. It was last seen losing height rapidly with smoke pouring from its engine. Sergeant R.C. Ford (R6611) followed MacKenzie through another stern attack before initiating an attack himself, from the beam. He then lost the bombers but spotted a Bf 110 making for cloud and opened fire at 400 yards shortly before it disappeared from view. On emerging from cloud himself, he

Spitfire Mk Is of No. 616 Squadron coming in to land. These two aircraft show different positioning of the under-wing roundel, X4330 has it at the tip, whereas the second machine has it further inboard. X4330 went on to fly with No. 457 Squadron and was written off at Grangemouth on 2 June 1942 with No. 58 OTU. *(Philip Jarrett)*

found that the 110 had turned the tables and was moving in to attack and he had to use violent evasive action to shake it off, eventually hiding in cloud before returning to base. The last member of Red section, Pilot Officer Eric Lock (R6885), attacked a Bf 110, setting its starboard motor on fire before three further short bursts caused its port engine to burst into flame. Return fire was experienced and Lock's Spitfire suffered two hits in the port wing (one through the main spar and one in the aileron). The 110 was last seen diving into cloud with both engines on fire.

In the meantime, Green and Blue sections had manoeuvred towards the escort fighters with Pilot Officer E.A. Shipman (N3126) ordering Green section into echelon port for a No. 3 attack on three Bf 110s. The Spitfires were spotted, however, and the Messerschmitts turned to face the attack, producing a brief head-on encounter, before the lead aircraft broke away to port at very close range. Shipman then went for another 110 with a series of deflection shots, followed by a stern attack that put its starboard engine out of action. It dived away, apparently out of control, and disappeared into cloud. Pilot Officer R.W. Wallens (N3266) half-rolled onto a Bf 110 and fired a two-second burst

at 100 yards. Although he saw his fire enter the aircraft he did not stop to observe its effect. Another 110 soon appeared and Wallens carried out a diving quarter attack giving up to a full ring deflection, pulling through the enemy from stern to nose with a three-second burst. Pieces flew off the 110, which went into a steep dive, leaving a column of thick blue-black smoke. Sergeant F. Usmar (N3162) fired at a Bf 110 that was on the tail of Wallens, but was then faced with an He 111 coming straight for him. A short burst caused the Heinkel to explode, the blast pitching Usmar's Spitfire violently upwards so that he temporarily lost control. Blue section also saw action and Pilot Officer A.D.J. 'Tony' Lovell (X4201) claimed one Bf 110 destroyed, with another probably destroyed.

The *Luftwaffe* raid, which had been aimed at a number of northern airfields, was also contested by No. 72 Squadron (Spitfires) aided by Nos 79, 605 and 607 Squadrons (Hurricanes). A total of

Spitfire Mk I X4179 of No. 19 Squadron. Note the elongated fabric patch over the middle two guns in place of individual covers. This aircraft survived until 24 October 1943, when it crashed on take-off from Eshott with No. 57 OTU. *(Philip Jarrett)*

Spitfire Mk VB AD233 of No. 222 Squadron shows the CO's pennant below the cockpit. It was lost on 25 May 1942 (along with its pilot Squadron Leader J.S. Jankiewiez) when shot down by an Fw 190A of I./JG 26 during Rodeo 51 to Ostend. *(Philip Jarrett)*

eight He 111s and six Bf 110s was shot down with another three 110s suffering damage, one being classified as a write-off on its return. No. 41 Squadron claimed four destroyed and five probables. Of the pilots taking part in this operation, Pilot Officer G.A. Langley was killed in action on 15 September 1940 in P9324 and Pilot Officers R.J. Boret, E.S. Lock, and O.B. Morrough-Ryan lost their lives later in the war.

As daylight attacks began to peter out towards the end of the year, any euphoria on the part of the British was tempered by the thought that it might only be a temporary reprieve. Whatever

lay in store, the demise of the Spitfire Mk III meant that it would be the 'interim' Mk V that would be the RAF's premier fighter in 1941. The new variant was introduced to service by No. 92 Squadron, the rest of the Biggin Hill Wing (Nos 74 and 609 Squadrons) beginning their conversion from Spitfire Mk IIs in May 1941. The transition was not without mishap, however, a number of propeller constant-speed

Spitfire Mk IB R7161 was converted to Mk VB standard in early April 1941, and flew with No. 92 Squadron at Biggin Hill. It was used by Pilot Officer Ronnie Fokes to destroy the Bf 109F of *Unteroffizier* Werner Zimmer (4./JG 53) on 26 April, and on 14 June it was flown by Squadron Leader Jamie Rankin when he shot down 13-kill ace *Leutnant* Robert Menge of I./JG 26. *(Peter R. Caygill)*

AB320 was the prototype Mk VB (trop) and was also used for manufacturer's trials with the 90-Imp gal slipper tank as seen here. It was eventually sent to the Middle East and was SOC on 27 April 1943. *(Philip Jarrett)*

unit (CSU) failures occurred at high altitude and there were problems with oxygen equipment. A combat report filed on 9 May by Flying Officer T.S. 'Wimpy' Wade of No. 92 Squadron (later chief test pilot at Hawker) highlights some of the difficulties experienced during high-altitude fighting: 'As YELLOW 1 I took off from Biggin Hill at 17:18 to patrol Maidstone at 15,000 ft. At about 18:24 when weaving above and behind the flight as the original weaver had passed out [oxygen starvation] and broken away, I sighted one 109 300 yards away climbing up to attack from astern. I immediately gave warning to the flight and proceeded to adopt violent action in an attempt to get on his tail. I completely iced up, however, and could see nothing, so went into a spiralling vertical dive to approximately 15,000 ft during which my ASI registered 440 mph. The Me 109 attempted to follow suit but in doing so broke his controls and the pilot baled out. When I eventually recovered normal flight I noticed I had been hit in the cannon ammunition drum on my starboard wing. I returned to base and landed, where I found glycol pouring out as cannon shell splinters had entered my glycol pipelines.'

The Circuses begin

For the first half of 1941 poor weather conditions meant that most operational flying consisted of defensive patrols with only occasional forays into France, but better conditions from mid-June allowed the fighting season to get under way in earnest, as recorded in the No. 609 Squadron Operational Record Book (ORB) for the 17th: 'After convoy patrols before lunch there began the first of that long series of Circuses [offensive operations involving bombers intended to draw *Luftwaffe* fighters into combat with the escorting fighters] which were to continue the rest of the summer. This was Circus 13, with Blenheims raiding Bethune, and 609 as part of the high cover escort at 25,000 ft in fours. Only three Me 109s were sighted near the target area, but on approaching the French coast on the way back, two or three pairs were sighted coming from the north. Blue section, at 20,000 ft north of Le Touquet, saw a pair below at 15,000 ft and dived on them. Flight Lieutenant Bisdee's cannons jammed, but with m.g. [machine-guns] only at short range, he caused one of the e/a [enemy aircraft] to go down "flaming like a torch". Flying Officer Ogilvie, using cannon and m.g., caused the other to "blow up with a great explosion" and land in the sea in flames. BLUE 3 (Pilot Officer de Spirlet) was in mid Channel at 12,000 ft when he saw a single Me 109 flying to his left on the same course. Both aircraft turned towards each other and Pilot Officer de

Spirlet opened fire from front quarter. He saw the e/a dive steeply, streaming black smoke from the fuselage. Squadron Leader Robinson saw a patch of frothing water in the position. He, Sergeant Hughes-Rees, Pilot Officer Atkinson, Sergeant Palmer and Pilot Officer Ortmans all fired as well.'

A period of hot, sunny weather which lasted, with only occasional breaks, until the end of July, allowed Fighter Command to operate one or more offensive missions over France on most days. One reason for the high level of activity was an attempt to tie down *Luftwaffe* fighter units to prevent them being transferred to the east to assist with the invasion of Russia which had been launched on 22 June. In the late afternoon of 9 August the Biggin Hill squadrons took part in a three-Wing Rodeo (fighter sweep) over northern France, one that was hotly contested. Squadron Leader Jamie Rankin's combat report gives a good indication of a typical fighter operation at that time: 'I was GARRICK LEADER [No. 92 Squadron], leading the Wing. R/v [rendezvous] was made with 609 Squadron over Gravesend at 17:35 and Wing climbed through 10/10 cloud over Kent. I flew south to establish position and managed to identify Dungeness through small gap in cloud. Height was then gained overland and the Wing arrived over Rye at 17:59 with squadrons at

24/25/30,000 ft. Kenley Wing could not be seen so one orbit was made and I set off at 18:03 without them. Wing crossed French coast between Boulogne and Hardelot at 18:12. One squadron of the Wing in front dived down almost immediately and at the same time I saw 8–12 109s coming from inland and turning round behind us from Le Touquet. I tried to get Knockout squadron [No. 72 Squadron] to attack and then my own Yellow section, but neither could spot them. I therefore attacked with Red section. The squadron split up into fours and was continuously engaged from then to 18:25. E/a were very numerous above, below and at same height and there was no difficulty in finding targets.

'Two formations of seven, which I chased with Red section, were caught and in both cases I hit 109Fs with cannon, HE (high explosive) strikes being visible. Later, at Gris Nez, when dogfighting with three 109s, I saw 10–12 more coming up and I ordered the section to dive out and the squadron to return to base. One 109F followed us down at more than 450 mph from

W3373 initially flew with No. 609 Squadron at Biggin Hill in the summer of 1941 and later served with Nos 154, 315, 317, 412, 349 and 303 Squadrons. It ended its days with No. 51 OTU and No. 1654 CU and was SOC on 10 September 1945. *(Philip Jarrett)*

2,000–1,000ft when he opened fire. I swung hard right and he overshot. Turning back onto him I fired from 10° deflection with m.g. only (cannon finished) and this e/a now at 500 ft tried to turn right whilst pulling out, and crashed into the sea, sending up a splash about 100 ft high. I then returned to base. Me 109s were much more inclined to stay and fight and the engagement in the Boulogne-St Omer area was one general dogfight. We could out turn the 109F easily but had not enough speed to close range when in a good position. R/T interference was experienced all the time over France and prevented me from bringing Knockout squadron, who were not engaged, into the melee.'

Fw 190 in theatre

A few days before this particular operation the Fw 190A-1s of *Oberleutnant* Otto Behrens' *Erprobungsstaffel* 190 had moved to Le Bourget from the *Luftwaffe* test facility at Rechlin to re-equip II./JG 26, and after a brief work-up period, transferred to Moorsele to begin operations over the Channel. The Fw 190 was beset by problems, mainly engine related, and although it had better performance than the Bf 109F, full advantage could not be taken until the snags were rectified.

By early 1942 many of the troubles had been overcome and its pilots were becoming more confident and much more aggressive. RAF Fighter Command had had a difficult enough time dealing with the Bf 109F in 1941, the introduction of the Fw 190A would lead to loss rates that, at times, were as severe as in the Battle of Britain. One pilot who lived through the 'Focke-Wulf summer' of 1942 was Squadron Leader C.F. 'Bunny' Currant, DSO, DFC, OC No. 501 Squadron. The following account refers to a combat in Spitfire Mk VB W3846 'SD-Z' that took place during Circus 113 on 9 March, a raid by six Bostons of No. 107 Squadron on the power station at Gosnay: 'We were at about 25,000 ft and in the melee I found myself alone with three Fw 190 fighters. It was an engagement from which I should never have survived. I knew that the Spitfire Mk V was no match for the 190s at height so I did a terminal dive, full throttle, having been hit once by one of them. My plan was to get to ground level as quickly as I could, so down I went with one bullet in my skull hurting like hell, and some of my instruments in dust. I hurtled down, pursued by all three, and each took a turn to fire at me from directly above (the Germans always seemed to use a lot of

A clipped-wing Spitfire LF.Mk VB of No. 118 Squadron. This photograph was probably taken between 19 June 1943, when No. 118's Mk VBs were converted to LF standard, and 19 September 1943, when the unit swapped aircraft with No. 64 Squadron and moved from Merston to Peterhead in Scotland. *(Philip Jarrett)*

Fine view of Spitfire Mk VB EN821 of No. 243 Squadron. It later flew with No. 65 Squadron before being issued to the Fleet Air Arm for use as a trainer at Lee-on-Solent in February 1944. *(Philip Jarrett)*

tracer which I could see very easily). At the end of the attacks, nothing had hit me. I reckon by then I must have been doing about 600 mph.

'In the middle of the vertical dive suddenly a remarkable thing happened – all three German fighters were below me. Unbeknown to them or me, my throttle had come loose and so my Spitfire slowed up rapidly. The Germans had no choice, they shot down past me and the hunted was now above and was the hunter. I was not feeling too well by then and could feel the blood running down my neck and back. I sprayed my bullets in their general direction and by then was below tree level. The three Focke-Wulfs were again behind me as I shot through a French farmyard at about 15 ft through a mass of cattle. I was conscious of cows' bums with tails up in the air and shit all over the place as well as Rhode Island Reds going past my wing tips. I thought they'd never again lay hard-shelled eggs!

'The Fw 190s turned inland and left me, and as I

was crossing the French coast I climbed hard to 10,000 ft in case I was forced to bale out. I got to Folkestone and saw Lympne airfield, tested my undercarriage and flaps and did a normal landing on the grass. Instantly the Spitfire did a huge somersault. The tyres had been hit by the first attack at height and I found myself upside down, parachute above me, and could hear the hiss of petrol pouring onto the hot engine. I could not get out but the fire-tender was there in a flash. I was taken to Folkestone hospital (the second time in two years I found myself in this same hospital). They gave me a local anaesthetic in my head and removed the German bullet. The day's events were extraordinary, a mixture of crisis and hilarity. I had one reaction when I felt that bullet

Spitfire Mk VBs of No. 340 Squadron raise the dust before take-off. 'GW-G' was most probably BL905. The Cross of Lorraine is carried on a shield just below the windscreen. *(Peter R. Caygill)*

hit my skull. I shouted "Oh God!" That was all. I was just so incredibly lucky.' In a postscript to this event, Currant had an X-ray taken in the 1980s when it was discovered that pieces of shrapnel were still embedded in his skull.

The superiority of the Fw 190A over the Spitfire Mk V was exacerbated by Fighter Command's attempt to take the initiative over northern France, which led to it suffering a similar fate to that of the *Luftwaffe* in 1940. Given adequate radar warning (which the Germans usually had) the fast-climbing 190s were able to get above the RAF formations and thus had tactical advantage as well as technical supremacy. Additionally there was the question of tactics. Even though there were a number of high-ranking officers on the RAF side who championed the use of the 'finger four' formation, many squadrons flew with each section in line astern in the traditional RAF manner. This was wasteful in terms of fuel (especially for those at the back) and the amount of cross-cover was minimal as everyone was playing follow the leader. Worse still, some squadrons were still using sections of three with weavers as late as mid-1942. This undoubtedly led to increased loss rates which during 1942 were in the order of 4:1 against.

Digby Wing

Although the Spitfire Mk IX entered service with No. 64 Squadron in July 1942, a year later there were still 21 fighter squadrons flying the Mk V in Nos 10, 11 and 12 Groups. Some had had their aircraft upgraded to LF.Mk VB standard by the fitting of cropped-blower Merlins. With increased performance at low level, the LF.Mk VB was still able to give a good account of itself. It was used to considerable effect in late 1943 by the Digby Wing which comprised Nos 402 and 416 Squadrons.

Situated to the south-east of Lincoln, Digby had long been regarded as a quiet backwater for rest and recuperation, but this was soon to change with the arrival of Squadron Leader Lloyd Chadburn to command No. 402 Squadron in May 1943. Shortly after, he was promoted to Wing Leader, Squadron Leader Geoff Northcott taking over No. 402, his opposite number on No. 416 being Squadron Leader F.E. Grant. Over the coming months the Digby Wing led something of a nomadic life which resulted in the Canadians' Spitfires operating anywhere from Holland to the Brest peninsula. Generally the Wing flew as close escort for medium bombers, but occasionally provided escort for Bristol Beaufighters carrying out shipping strikes off the Dutch coast. Although the *Luftwaffe* was being put under extreme pressure the chances of combat were still high, and on 3 November the Digby Wing had its most successful day of the year during Ramrod 290 (Ramrods saw groups of bombers or fighter-bombers tasked against a particular target), an attack by 72 Martin B-26 Marauders on the airfield at Schiphol.

On the return journey a gaggle of around 15 Bf 109Gs of II./JG 3 made a somewhat half-hearted attempt to get behind the lead bombers, but were prevented from doing so by No. 402 Squadron, engagements continuing for the next 15 minutes from the coast to approximately 18 miles offshore. Lloyd Chadburn (RED 1) dispatched two Messerschmitt Bf 109s in quick succession and in the short gap between each combat saw three other aircraft going down in flames and two parachutes. Geoff Northcott in the meantime was leading his section onto the second pair, firing a burst 30° off on the port side of one of the 109s, which caused it to disintegrate in flames.

By now the Messerschmitts had been split up and were in complete disarray. Flight Lieutenant John Mitchner noticed a lone 109 coming in behind the bombers but was unable to open fire as it took violent evasive action, turning steeply left and right. Suddenly it straightened out, and just as Mitchner was closing in for the kill, he saw the hood fly off and the pilot bale out.

Squadron Leader Neville Duke, DSO, DFC warms up Spitfire Mk VC LZ978 before take-off from Abu Sueir, Egypt. Duke was Chief Flying Instructor (CFI) at No. 73 OTU, Abu Sueir from 11 June 1943 to 27 February 1944. Note the white-painted wing tips. *(Neville Duke via author)*

Looking back, he observed another melee about five miles away and quickly joined in. He had no difficulty closing on another 109 and fired several short bursts which struck the forward fuselage, its pilot also taking to his parachute.

At the head of No. 416 Squadron's Green section, Flight Lieutenant Art Sager dived onto four 109s, two of which broke away to head inland, Sager attacking the right-hand Messerschmitt while his wingman, Flying Officer W.H. Jacobs, went for the other. A short burst damaged the 109, but a cannon stoppage then made aiming impossible. His attack was taken up, however, by Flight Lieutenant Dan Noonan, who secured further hits, the German crashing in flames on the outskirts of Zandvoort. Sager then pulled up to witness the aircraft that had been attacked by Jacobs coming down a short distance away, but it was clear that his

Spitfire Mk VC EP193 'QJ-U' of No. 92 Squadron, in North Africa in early 1943. No. 92 Squadron markings showed a fair amount of variety around this period and are seen here with the 'QJ' squadron identifier in toned-down grey. *(Neville Duke via author)*

Another No. 92 Squadron Spitfire Mk VC (EP442) with just the vaguest hint of 'QJ' code letters to the right of the fuselage roundel. When No. 92 Squadron moved on to the Mk IX, it flew for a time with numerals instead of code letters. *(Neville Duke via author)*

No. 2 had been hit as his Spitfire was pouring glycol. He did not return.

Following his initial victory, Noonan climbed steeply up to 2,000 ft, where he saw a solitary 109 approaching from the west. It flew towards him and tried to get on his tail by turning steeply, but when this failed the pilot cut his throttle in an attempt to make Noonan overshoot. Despite this, the Canadian was able to out-manoeuvre his opponent quite easily and fired several bursts from 100 yards, securing hits all over the fuselage. The cockpit hood flew off, but before the pilot could bale out the 109 flicked onto its back and dived vertically into the ground. The final combat involved Flight Lieutenant Doug Booth of No. 416 Squadron: 'I was leading White section as we escorted the

Wing Commander Ian Gleed's personal Spitfire Mk VC, AB502, near the North African coast in early 1943. As the leader of No. 244 Wing, Gleed had his aircraft marked with his individual code letters 'IR-G' and a 'Figaro' motif under the windscreen. Gleed was shot down and killed in this aircraft on 16 April 1943, possibly by *Leutnant* Ernst-Wilhelm Reinart of JG 77. At the time of his death Gleed had 13 victories with another three shared. *(Philip Jarrett)*

Clipped-wing LF.Mk VB EP688 features an Aboukir filter, and is seen in August 1943 at Gerbini in Sicily in the markings of No. 40 (SAAF) Squadron. It has an opening in the fuselage side (covered over) for an F.24 camera, as befitting the unit's tactical reconnaissance role. *(Philip Jarrett)*

third box of bombers away from the target and headed for home. We had crossed out over the enemy coast and there was a lot of chatter on the R/T as the forward echelons were obviously in a scrap. I spotted three Bf 109s approaching from the sea about 1,000 ft below. I peeled off to port and dove to attack. As I closed, the 109 took evasive action while diving to the deck. I fired several short bursts and then it levelled out before suddenly half-rolling and diving into the sea. I wondered if they were heading back to base, out of ammo. In any event I think they were caught by surprise, not expecting us coming from the land.'

Of those shot down, Flying Officer Jacobs was killed when his aircraft (BL430) crashed near Zandvoort, and on the German side five pilots were killed including the *Kommodore* of II./JG 3, Major Kurt Brandle. Although two wings of Spitfire Mk VBs fought at the time of D-Day (Deanland and Horne) the mark had largely been withdrawn from front-line duties by the end of the year, although some soldiered on with Air-Sea Rescue (ASR) squadrons. The last time a Mk V fired its guns in anger was most probably on 12 March 1945, when Flight Lieutenant K.S. Butterfield of No. 276 Squadron sank a German 'Biber'-class midget submarine in the Scheldt estuary.

Mediterranean service

The Spitfire Mk V was used extensively in the Mediterranean from 1942, the first aircraft arriving in Malta on 7 March. Spitfires were urgently needed to replace slow-climbing Hurricanes and by the end of October the aerial siege had been broken. Space does not allow anything other than a brief look at the battle to save Malta but the activities of 6 June were typical of many. The day began with a dawn patrol by Spitfires of No. 185 Squadron which were vectored onto a Ju 88. The bomber was soon attacked by Flight Sergeants H. Haggas and J.E. McNamara. Two more Ju 88s were set upon by a section from No. 249 Squadron led by Flight Lieutenant P.B. 'Laddie' Lucas, who claimed one of the Junkers (shared with Pilot Officer Frank Jones), the other falling to a combined attack by Pilot Officer 'Ossie' Linton and Flight Sergeant 'Micky' Butler.

An hour later No. 249 Squadron was in action again, four of its Spitfires, together with eleven from No. 603 Squadron, being directed towards an Italian raid on Safi by five Cant Z.1007bis bombers with an escort of 24 Macchi MC.202s and 12 Reggiane Re.2001s. Warrant Officer C.B. 'Chuck' Ramsay and Sergeant Johnny Gilbert each claimed a Reggiane, although only one was actually lost, that flown by *Tenente* Leonardo Venturini of 358ª *Squadriglia*. One of the Cants was also damaged. Pilot Officer Wally McLeod's Spitfire was hit, but he made a successful dead-stick landing on return. A third 'raid' appeared on the radar screens at 09:20 but this turned out to be Re.2001s, looking for Venturini. The Italians were bounced by four Spitfires of No. 249 Squadron, Flying Officer Raoul Daddo-Langlois and Pilot Officer Frank Jones both claiming one Re.2001 destroyed. Again only one was lost (*Tenente* Arnaldo De Merich of 152ª *Squadriglia*), the other, flown by *Capitano* Salvatore Teia, making it back to crash-land at Comiso.

Another ASR operation carried out by the Italians in the afternoon led to further activity when two sections of four Spitfires from No. 185 Squadron attacked around 20 Re.2001s and MC.202s protecting a Cant Z.506B floatplane. Flight Lieutenant Johnny Plagis shot down two Re.2001s, with another being claimed by Flight Sergeant D.G. 'Shorty' Reid. Once again there was some overclaiming as only two Re.2001s of 152ª *Squadriglia* were lost, those flown by *Tenente*

Giuseppe Baraldi and *Sergente Maggiore* Aldo Geminiani. In the meantime, some pilots were in a quandary over what to do about the Z.506B 'blood wagon' (as Plagis put it) but their indecision was brought to an end when it was blasted from the sky by the three Canadians of Blue Section, Pilot Officer J.F. Lambert, Flight Sergeant W.G. Dodd and Sergeant H.R. Russel. After dark two Spitfires were scrambled to intercept a raid on Luqa but were unable to make contact.

North African operations

Spitfires were also desperately required in North Africa and the first to see action were those of No. 145 Squadron in June 1942 during Rommel's summer offensive. By the time of El Alamein on 23 October, Nos 92 and 601 Squadrons were also operational in theatre and had joined No. 145 Squadron to form No. 244 Wing. Once the line had been broken the German retreat was rapid and very soon attention was centred on the landings in Morocco and Algeria. Following Operation *Torch* another seven squadrons of Spitfire Mk VCs became operational in North Africa (Nos 72, 81, 93, 111, 152, 154 and 242) and these were joined by the similarly equipped 31st and 52nd Fighter Groups of the USAAF. Initially the tactical air forces had difficulty operating due to the poor state of airfields in the area, but come the new year, better weather allowed Allied air power to overwhelm the overstretched fighter units of the

Two clipped-wing Spitfire Mk VBs of the 31st Fighter Group, USAAF in 1943. Formerly assigned to the 8th Air Force, the Group's Spitfires were dispatched to Gibraltar by ship in October 1942 and fought in North Africa and Italy with the 12th Air Force until May 1944, when the unit re-equipped with Mustangs. *(Philip Jarrett)*

Spitfire Mk VB (trop) 5512 of the Turkish Air Force, one of 63 Mk VBs supplied to Turkey in 1944–45. They were in service, along with a number of Fw 190As acquired from Germany, until 1948–49. *(Peter R. Caygill)*

Luftwaffe and *Regia Aeronautica*. During the next three months the top-scoring pilot in this theatre was Flying Officer Neville Duke, DFC, who had rejoined No. 92 Squadron on 18 November 1942, having previously flown with the unit in 1941 when it was part of the Biggin Hill Wing. By the end of March he had shot down a further 12 German and Italian aircraft. Having already disposed of two MC.202s and three Bf 109Fs in the first four days of March, Duke made it seven on the 7th, as his combat reports testify:

'0800: Medenine: Leading a sweep of six aircraft on patrol of forward troops at 17,000 ft over Medenine, saw three Me 109s flying east in line abreast at 15,000 ft, five miles east of squadron. Squadron turned about and dived on the 109s. I closed on the port 109 and observed strikes on the fuselage as enemy aircraft turned; with second burst enemy aircraft seemed to lurch violently. The aircraft went down in a wide spiral dive as if the pilot was hit, and crashed. The enemy aircraft did not explode on the ground. Claim one Me 109F destroyed.

'14:50: near Noffiata : I led four aircraft on a scramble from Hazbub at 10,000 ft and engaged 5+ Me 109Fs above us. The enemy aircraft dived east and I followed, firing bursts at one 109 on which I observed strikes. At 6,000 ft over Noffiata aerodrome I was engaged with numerous 109s. I closed to 100 yards astern of enemy aircraft and observed top of tail, hood and large pieces of fuselage disintegrate. The aircraft caught fire and the pilot baled out. Claim one Me 109F destroyed.'

After the defeat of Axis forces in North Africa, preparations were made for the invasion of Sicily which began on 10 July 1943, to be followed two months later by landings in Italy. Even at this late stage Spitfire Mk VCs were still in the majority and were the equipment of ten squadrons (Nos 43, 72, 92, 152, 232, 242, 243, 417, 601, RAF and No. 1, SAAF). In addition the USAAF's 31st and 52nd Fighter Groups flew Spitfire Mk Vs and continued to do so until converting to North American P-51 Mustangs in April 1944. By this time many RAF squadrons had also re-equipped with Spitfire Mk VIIIs and Mk IXs.

Far Eastern Spitfires

Spitfire Mk VCs were also flown in northern Australia by No. 54 Squadron together with Nos 452 and 457 (RAAF) Squadrons, to counter Japanese raids on Darwin and the surrounding area. The change of environment unfortunately led to numerous technical difficulties that

A Spitfire PR.Mk IV in Russian markings. In September 1942 a detachment of three PR.Mk IVs of No. 1 PRU, under Flight Lieutenant E.A. Fairhurst, left for Vaenga in northern Russia where it was to monitor German Naval activity that was disrupting Arctic convoys. One aircraft was lost on 27 September and the aircraft illustrated is most probably one of the remaining two Spitfires left behind when the flight returned in November 1942. *(Philip Jarrett)*

seriously inhibited the aircraft's effectiveness, most of the problems being caused by large temperature variations with hot and humid conditions at ground level and extreme cold at high altitude. A spate of CSU failures harked back to the introduction of the Mk V in 1941 and a series of glycol leaks and engine failures resulted in more aircraft being lost in accidents than to enemy action. Operations commenced in January 1943 and despite numerous setbacks the Japanese incursions were blunted, in particular flights by Mitsubishi Ki-46 'Dinah' reconnaissance aircraft, that had previously enjoyed freedom from interception. The top-scoring pilot in the Australian theatre was Wing Commander Clive 'Killer' Caldwell, who claimed eight Japanese aircraft destroyed. Spitfire Mk VCs were also used against the Japanese in Burma by Nos 136, 607 and 615 Squadrons, RAF until Spitfire Mk VIIIs became available around April 1944.

Exported aircraft

Early-mark Spitfires were used by a number of foreign air forces. Although interest in the Mk I was widespread, the declaration of war limited exports to three examples for Turkey (Type 341 –

P9566 and P9567) plus L1066, which had been intended for Poland, and one for France. Later in the war 13 Spitfire Mk Is (Type 336) were delivered to Portugal. The Spitfire Mk V was exported much more widely and eventually flew with the air forces of France, Russia, Portugal, Greece, Turkey, Yugoslavia, India, Egypt, Italy and South Africa. Single examples were also acquired by Denmark, Norway, Belgium and Czechoslovakia. A batch was delivered to Australia but the largest user outside the RAF and Fleet Air Arm (FAA) was the USAAF.

On 29 September 1942 the three 'Eagle' squadrons (Nos 71, 121 and 133) were disbanded and incorporated into the USAAF as the 334th, 335th and 336th Pursuit Squadrons of the 4th Fighter Group based at Debden. Operations with Spitfire Mk VBs continued until March 1943, when the Group converted to the Republic P-47 Thunderbolt. The Spitfire Mk V was also flown by the 31st Fighter Group (307th, 308th and 309th Fighter Squadrons) and the 52nd Fighter Group (2nd, 4th and 5th Fighter Squadrons), both Groups being assigned to the 12th Air Force in September 1942 for combat in the wake of Operation *Torch*.

3. Engineers and Aces

Reginald J. Mitchell: designer

The name of Reginald J. Mitchell will be remembered principally as being that of the man who created the Spitfire and thus delivered to Britain one of the means by which it retained its freedom in the desperate air battles of 1940. Mitchell was born on 20 May 1895 in Stoke-on-Trent and although he showed a flair for art at school, his main interest was in engineering. In 1911 he was apprenticed to Kerr Stuart, a locomotive engineering firm, which quickly recognised his talent and offered him work in the company drawing office. Mitchell stayed with Kerr Stuart until 1916 when he joined

Pemberton-Billing Ltd at Southampton. The company became Supermarine Aviation two years later. In 1919 he was appointed Chief Designer and embarked on a career that would see him be responsible for 24 designs, commencing with the Sea Lion II that won the Schneider Trophy for Britain in 1922. Although Mitchell designed such classic flying-boats as the Southampton and Stranraer, before the Spitfire

Superb view of the Spitfire prototype K5054, in its original form with stub exhausts and small wheel doors to the undercarriage legs. Also apparent from this angle is the coarse pitch of the two-bladed wooden propeller. *(Philip Jarrett)*

he was known principally for his elegant Schneider racers, the S.4, S.5 and S.6.

The first in the series, the S.4, was a revolutionary cantilever monoplane powered by a 680-hp Napier Lion VII. It was flown for the first time on 24 August 1925 by Henri Biard, but crashed during pre-race testing for the 1925 Schneider contest in Baltimore, USA, due to wing flutter. The follow-up S.5 was of similar configuration (but possessing a wire-braced wing) and won the 1927 contest in Venice at a speed of 281.65 mph. By now the Napier Lion engine was reaching the end of its development potential and a new engine was needed for the S.6 that was to represent Britain in the 1929 contest. Complacency at Napier was countered by enthusiasm at Rolls-Royce, and the company's R (Racing) engine was built in six months to power Mitchell's design to victory at Calshot. The Schneider Trophy was won outright in 1931 by Flight Lieutenant J.N. Boothman in an S.6B powered by a 2,350-hp Rolls-Royce R engine.

Just two years after the Schneider triumph R.J. Mitchell was diagnosed as having cancer of the rectum and had to undergo an operation in 1933.

At this time the Type 224 to Specification F.7/30 was taking shape, but Mitchell's thoughts soon turned to a more advanced design utilising the new Rolls-Royce PV.12 engine. This design became the Spitfire. Despite continuing health concerns, Mitchell worked relentlessly to see his design come to fruition but his condition deteriorated and he died on 11 June 1937. The Spitfire was to be his legacy and it was left to his team at Supermarine to realise its potential. That team had comprised Assistant Chief Designer Major Harold Payne, head of the Technical Office Alan Clifton, aerodynamicist Beverley Shenstone, Chief Draughtsman Joseph Smith, flight test controller Ernie Mansbridge and with 'Mutt' Summers as Chief Test Pilot. With Mitchell gone it would be up to Joe Smith, his replacement as Chief Designer, and Alan Clifton, to ensure that the Spitfire became a classic.

At Rolls-Royce another team was busy with the engine that was to power the early-mark Spitfires. In the early 1920s Rolls had nearly quit aero engine manufacture to concentrate on car production, but the need for a V-12 liquid-cooled engine to rival the American-designed Curtiss D-12 of the Fairey Fox two-seat day bomber

The first production Spitfire Mk I K9787. This aircraft was used for various trials, including assessments of spinning and dive performance by the A&AEE at Martlesham Heath in October 1938 (see Chapter 4). It was eventually converted as a PR.Mk IC for use by the PRU, and failed to return on 30 June 1941. *(Philip Jarrett)*

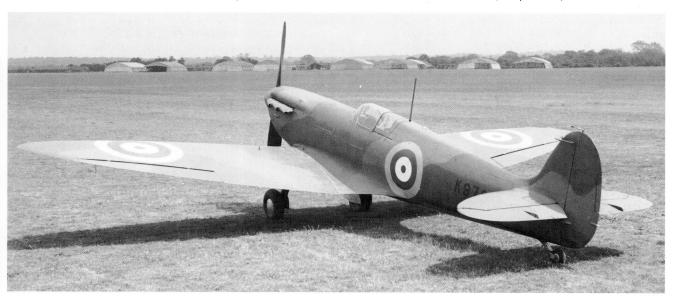

This anonymous Spitfire Mk I has black/white undersides, but only to the wings. Although the Air Ministry requested the dividing line between black and white be along the fuselage centreline, Supermarine delivered a number of aircraft as shown. *(Philip Jarrett)*

(together with indifference at Napier) prompted them to return with renewed vigour. The Rolls-Royce F was developed into the Kestrel and the larger H became the Buzzard. Although only 100 of the latter were produced, it formed the basis for the R racing engine. Having compressed about five years' engine development into six months for the Schneider contest, the way was now open for the design of a new engine to succeed the Kestrel, the PV.12.

At the time of the PV.12's inception, Rolls's hierarchy was split between West Wittering in Sussex – the home of Sir Henry Royce, and the main works in Derby. Chief Engineer A.G. Elliott worked in close collaboration with Royce and at Derby, Ernest Hives had assembled a core of engineers, some of whom were to serve the company throughout the war and for many years after. Chief among these were Colonel T.B. Barrington and Arthur Rubbra, who took on the design responsibility for the PV.12 with Jimmy Ellor and Cyril Lovesey as experimental engineers. With the death of Royce on 22 April 1933, Elliott returned full time to Derby. Progress on what would become the Merlin was such that the engine was first bench-run on 15 October and flight testing at Hucknall, under Ray Dorey

and Harry Pearson, got under way in April 1935 using a Hawker Hart. In early 1938 Rolls acquired the services of Stanley Hooker, whose first job was to increase the efficiency of the Merlin supercharger, thereby increasing its power by around 30 per cent.

Jeffrey Kindersley Quill: test pilot

When one considers the many pilots connected with the Spitfire, one name stands out above all others, Jeffrey Kindersley Quill. Born on 1 February 1913 at Littlehampton in Sussex, Quill was educated at Lancing College from 1926-31, before joining the RAF. His *ab initio* training was on Avro Tutors at No. 3 Flying Training School, Grantham where he also undertook advanced flying on the Armstrong Whitworth Siskin Mk IIIA. With the pilot rating 'Exceptional' stamped in his logbook, he was posted to No. 17 Squadron at Upavon to fly Bristol Bulldogs. At Grantham Quill had shown a natural aptitude for instrument flying and his next posting was to the Meteorological Flight at Duxford, where he became its CO in November 1934. Back on Siskins, he had the misfortune to crash-land on 14 March 1935 in marginal weather conditions, this resulting in the almost

Spitfire Mk Is of Hornchurch-based No. 65 Squadron in mid-1939. 'FZ-L' is K9906 flown by Flight Lieutenant Bob Stanford Tuck. Close examination of the original print shows K9906 still to be fitted with a ring and bead sight. *(Philip Jarrett)*

inevitable 'Siskin nose' which only served to aggravate a condition acquired earlier while boxing for the RAF. Quill's name was already being spoken about elsewhere, however, and at the end of 1935 he left the RAF to become assistant to 'Mutt' Summers at Vickers.

On 5 March 1936 Quill flew Summers to Eastleigh in the company's Miles Falcon, so that Summers could carry out the first flight in the F.37/34 fighter. Quill did not have to wait long to fly it himself and carried out his own maiden flight in K5054 on the 26th. Over the next 12 years Quill flew every version of the Spitfire, right up to the Seafire Mk 47 in 1946, his incomparable ability as a test pilot ensuring that aircraft delivered for service did not possess any hidden flaw to trap the unwary. Such was his dedication that he managed to secure a posting to No. 65 Squadron at Hornchurch during the Battle of Britain, to obtain operational

experience so as to appreciate more fully the requirements demanded of the Spitfire and to find ways of eradicating its few shortcomings. That, at least, was the line that he used to convince his employers to let him go: another motive lay in a deep desire to fight for his country. On 16 August he shot down a Bf 109E and two days later shared in the destruction of an He 111. Quill was Chief Test Pilot at Supermarine until 1947 when he was forced to retire on medical grounds. Thereafter he undertook various ground-based tasks within Vickers and BAC, which culminated in the role of Director of Marketing at Panavia. He died on 20 February 1996.

Alex Henshaw: test pilot

Another name synonymous with the Spitfire is that of Alex Henshaw, whose career as a production and development test pilot at Castle Bromwich saw him fly 2,360 Spitfires, approximately 10 per cent of the total number produced. Henshaw had achieved fame in the 1930s as a racing and record-breaking pilot, his most famous flight being the dash to Cape Town and back in Percival Mew Gull G-AEXF in

February 1939. Following a short spell at Vickers, he transferred to Castle Bromwich in the summer of 1940 as its Chief Test Pilot. Production testing usually involved a short flight to check for accurate stick-free trim, followed by power checks at rated altitude and a dive to maximum IAS to ensure the aircraft did not have any undesirable qualities when flown at its limiting speed. If time allowed, aerobatics would also be performed to assess an individual aircraft's handling characteristics. During his six years as a test pilot, Henshaw probably got to know the Spitfire Mk II and Mk V (and Mk IX) better than anyone and his aerobatic displays have achieved legendary status.

The aces

Of the thousands of service pilots that flew the Spitfire in World War Two only an extremely small proportion were to have the necessary skills and luck to become an ace. As Air Chief Marshal Sir Hugh Dowding, Fighter Command's C-in-C, had deliberately withheld his Spitfire squadrons from involvement in France, it was not until the evacuation of Dunkirk that his most prized asset was thrown into the fray. It was from this time that pilots of the calibre of 'Sailor' Malan, Bob Stanford Tuck, Colin Gray and Al Deere began their long and successful careers; others were to shine just as brightly but have since been largely forgotten.

Eric Stanley Lock

Of the early-mark Spitfire pilots, the fourth-highest scoring ace (after Malan, Beurling and Finucane) was Eric Stanley Lock from Shrewsbury. Having joined the RAFVR (RAF Volunteer Reserve) in 1939, Lock was called up at the outbreak of war and eventually posted to No. 41 Squadron at Catterick in August 1941. By the end of the month No. 41 Squadron was based at Hornchurch and within four weeks Lock had increased his score to 17, resulting in a well-earned DFC.

Four more kills (all Bf 109Es) followed in

Line-up of Spitfire Mk Is of No. 19 Squadron at Duxford probably taken on press day, 4 May 1939. The aircraft show Type B roundels (red centre and blue surround) on their upper wings and fuselage. The underwing roundels were deleted. *(Philip Jarrett)*

October and he received a Bar to his DFC only three weeks after the initial award. His final claims of the year were two Bf 109Es shot down over the Thames Estuary on 17 November, but he in turn was attacked from behind by a Bf 109 of JG 54 and wounded in the right arm and both legs. During a crash-landing at Martlesham Heath his Spitfire (P7554) overturned and he was trapped for two hours until released. A long and painful stay in hospital saw him undergo 15 operations for shrapnel to be removed from his limbs and he was not able to return to operations until July 1941, when he joined No. 611 Squadron as a flight commander, having also received a DSO. On 3 August he was engaged on a Rhubarb sortie over France in W3257 and was last seen attacking German soldiers near Calais.

John Webster

One of Lock's comrades at No. 41 Squadron was Flight Lieutenant John Webster from Liverpool, who had joined the RAF in 1935 on a short service commission. By the start of the war he was a flight commander and recorded his first victory over Dunkirk on 31 May 1940 when he shot down a Bf 109E. Webster's score began to increase during the early stages of the Battle of Britain and on 8 August he shot down three Bf 109Es and shared in the destruction of another. At the end of the month he was awarded a DFC, but was dead within a week. In combat near Basildon on 5 September, his aircraft (R6635) collided with P9428, flown by his CO, Squadron Leader H.R.L. Hood, and both pilots were killed. At the time of his death, Webster's score stood at 12 destroyed.

A Spitfire Mk I of No. 609 Squadron at Drem in late 1939 or early 1940. This aircraft still has the original radio mast, but bulletproof glazing has been fitted to the windscreen. It also has black under the port wing only and not to the fuselage undersides. *(Eric Watson via author)*

Bill Franklin

Pilot Officer Bill Franklin of No. 65 Squadron was another to score his first victory at Dunkirk, indeed he was one of the most successful pilots during this period, with three confirmed destroyed and three shared. Franklin was from East London and was considerably older than his fellow pilots, having joined the RAF in the late 1920s as a Halton apprentice. He was to become something of a Bf 109 specialist and shot down ten during the Battle of Britain, leading to the award of a DFM and Bar, followed shortly after by a commission. Sadly, he did not live to see out the year. On 12 December his was one of four Spitfires scrambled to intercept a Ju 88 carrying out a reconnaissance off Selsey Bill and both he and Sergeant M.H.E. Hine succumbed to its defensive fire.

Paterson Hughes

Of the many Commonwealth pilots that fought in the RAF, Flight Lieutenant Paterson Hughes was one of the brightest stars. Born on 19 September 1917 in Cooma, New South Wales, he joined the RAAF before embarking for Britain and the RAF. Posted initially to No. 64 Squadron at Church Fenton, he was soon transferred to the newly formed No. 234 Squadron at Leconfield as a flight commander, arriving on 8 November 1939. By July 1940, No. 234 Squadron was in No. 10 Group at St Eval and on the 8th Hughes shared in No. 234's first victory, a Ju 88 shot down off Land's End. In mid-August the squadron moved to Middle Wallop, where it was in action daily, and on the 16th Hughes shot down two Bf 109Es, one of which blew up with such force that he felt the jolt in his own machine.

Multiple scores became Hughes's forte, as two more 109s were destroyed on both the 18th and the 26th. On 4 September, however, he went one better and shot down three. On this occasion his victims were Bf 110s that had formed a defensive circle, but Hughes's tactic was to fly around the circle from the opposite direction. Three bursts set the lead Messerschmitt on fire and another dived vertically to crash near Tangmere. Hughes then attacked a third 110 and after following it down, saw it crash into the Channel. Three more 109s were dispatched in the next two days before he was involved in combat with a Dornier Do 17 on 7 September. One reason for his success was a predilection for attacking from close range and it may have been this that led to his downfall. Hughes's attack destroyed the Dornier, but another member of his section reported seeing his aircraft (X4009) going down with part of its wing missing. His aircraft might have been hit by debris, although others have suggested that he was shot down in error by a Hurricane. Hughes's final score was 14 destroyed with three shared and the award of a DFC was gazetted after his death.

Battle of Britain aces

The hectic pace of the Battle of Britain made heroes of many others. Pilot Officer George Bennions of No. 41 Squadron had 12 confirmed kills before he was shot down on 1 October in X4559. Badly wounded in the head, he lost an eye and like many others had to undergo plastic surgery. New Zealander Pilot Officer Brian Carbury of No. 603 Squadron was the second-highest-scoring Spitfire pilot of the Battle (after Lock), claiming 15 victories plus one shared (including five Bf 109Es in one day on 31 August), and another Auxiliary, Squadron Leader John Ellis of No. 610 Squadron, secured ten kills including three Bf 109Es shot down near Folkstone on 25 July. A comrade of Paterson Hughes, Pilot Officer Bob Doe of No. 234 Squadron was credited with eleven victories in Spitfires before being posted to No. 238 Squadron on Hurricanes, his score being matched by No. 609 Squadron's Flight Lieutenant John Dundas, whose final victim was *Major* Helmut Wick, *Kommodore* of JG 2, on 28 November. Within seconds Dundas was himself shot down and killed by *Leutnant* Rudi Pflanz, Wick's No. 2.

Other top-scoring Spitfire pilots in the Battle of Britain were Pilot Officer Colin Gray (15 victories) of No. 54 Squadron, Sergeant Andrew McDowall (11) of No. 602 Squadron, Flying Officer John 'Pancho' Villa (10) who flew with

A hive of activity surrounds this No. 19 Squadron Spitfire Mk I at Fowlmere during the Battle of Britain. Blown fabric patches show that the guns have been fired and the armourers are hard at work changing empty ammunition boxes. Replacement boxes are in the wooden carriers. *(Philip Jarrett)*

A dramatic scene from the film 'First of the Few' which was partially shot at Ibsley in late 1941. Although the aircraft in the foreground wears the codes of No. 501 Squadron, it is actually Mk II P8789 of No. 118 Squadron, a presentation Spitfire that carried the title *Borough of Wanstead and Woodford*. The real 'SD-E' is being flown by Flight Lieutenant C.F. 'Bunny' Currant in the background. P8789 went on to fly with No. 65 Squadron and was lost on 1 June 1942. *(C.F. Currant via author)*

Nos 72 and 92 Squadrons and Flying Officer Des McMullen (10) of Nos 54 and 222 Squadrons. Several other pilots also claimed ten kills, including No. 92 Squadron's Flight Lieutenant Bob Stanford Tuck, Pilot Officer George 'Grumpy' Unwin of No. 19 Squadron and Pilot Officer Ronald 'Ras' Berry of No. 603 Squadron.

Aces on the offensive

Come 1941, Dowding and Park had been replaced by Sholto Douglas and Leigh-Mallory as commanders of Fighter Command and No. 11 Group respectively, and the new hierarchy presided over a move from defence to attack with the launch of Circus operations and fighter sweeps over France. Several veterans from the previous year had further success, notably 'Sailor' Malan (first incumbent to the newly created post of Wing Commander (Flying)) whose score increased to 29 plus seven shared as leader of the Biggin Hill Wing, whilst at Tangmere, Douglas Bader led the Wing in his own inimitable style and achieved 9½ Spitfire victories to add to his single kill over Dunkirk, before he was shot down and captured on 9 August. At Hornchurch the Wing was frequently led by station commander Group Captain Harry Broadhurst, who had a highly

Supermarine-built Spitfire Mk VB W3759 was first flown at Eastleigh on 9 August 1941 and served with Nos 129, 316, 306 and 350 Squadrons. It later flew with No. 53 OTU and was SOC on 5 October 1945. *(Philip Jarrett)*

Spitfire Mk VB (trop) BL676, carried the presentation title *Bondowoso* and was converted by Air Service Training (AST) at Hamble as the first Seafire Mk IB MB328 in January 1942. *(Philip Jarrett)*

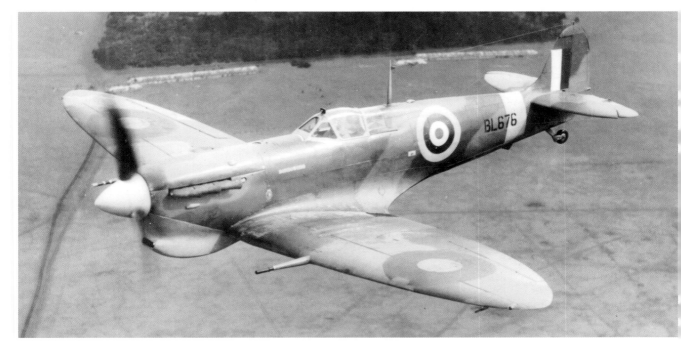

successful summer, claiming ten kills. However, all of the above-mentioned pilots were eclipsed by a 20-year-old Irishman, Flight Lieutenant Brendan 'Paddy' Finucane.

Brendan 'Paddy' Finucane

A devout Roman Catholic, Finucane was born in Dublin and moved with his family to Richmond, Surrey before joining the RAF in 1938. His first posting was to No. 65 Squadron, initial combat successes comprising two Bf 109Es shot down during the Battle of Britain. In April 1941 he became a flight commander with No. 452 Squadron, the first Australian fighter squadron to form in the UK, and by July the unit was declared operational. Once the fighting season got under way in earnest Finucane's score began to rise rapidly, his (and the squadron's) most successful day occurring on 16 August when he claimed three Bf 109Es out of a squadron total of seven during two operations, a sweep from Dunkirk to Gravelines and a Circus (No. 74) to the airfield at Marquise. By the end of the year his score had risen to 21, with three more shared, resulting in the award of a DFC and two Bars and a DSO. In January 1942 Finucane was given command of No. 602 Squadron at Kenley, but soon after was wounded in the thigh and arm during combat with an Fw 190. Although he was able to return to Kenley, he passed out through loss of blood immediately after landing. By early June his score had risen to 26 plus six shared and on the 27th he was appointed Hornchurch Wing Leader. Just over two weeks later, on 15 July, his Spitfire Mk VB (BM308) was hit by ground fire

during a Rhubarb sortie. Rather than bale out he attempted to get back to base but was forced to ditch in the Channel, his aircraft sinking before he was able to get out.

The Biggin Hill Wing

The top-scoring Wing in 1941 was that at Biggin Hill. Following the departure of 'Sailor' Malan in August, the Wing was led at first by the ebullient Micky Robinson of No. 609 Squadron, but when he became tour-expired it was taken over by No. 92 Squadron's Jamie Rankin. Although he had come to No. 92 with minimal combat experience, Rankin was to be one of the top-scoring pilots of the year and was to introduce a style of leadership somewhat different to that of Malan. The tough South African had had a reputation for being extremely aggressive in the air and as he was always liable to break without warning, his wingmen had a tough time staying with him. Rankin was altogether different, his Wing flying was immaculate and he had much greater thought for his No. 2, which made life a good deal easier for some of his junior pilots. His final total of 17 destroyed with five shared made him the sixth-highest-scoring ace on early-mark Spitfires.

Three places below Rankin was another No. 92 Squadron pilot, Flight Sergeant Don Kingaby. A former clerk in an insurance office, Kingaby had flown in the Battle of Britain with No. 266 Squadron but it was not until he joined No. 92 that his true abilities as a fighter pilot came to the fore. His greatest day had occurred on 15 November 1940 when he claimed three Bf 109Es and a probable in two sorties, and he continued be one of Fighter Command's top scorers during 1941. Renowned for his shooting ability, he also had luck on his side at times, none more so than on 2 July. During a sweep over the Channel, two aircraft dived past his section which he initially thought were Hurricanes, but which were in fact 109s acting

Sergeant Frank Jones (RCAF) of No. 72 Squadron aboard Spitfire Mk VB W3320, *The Darlington Spitfire*, at Gravesend in November 1941. Jones was posted to No. 249 Squadron on Malta in May 1942 and was credited with four aircraft destroyed plus two shared. During this time he was promoted to Flight Lieutenant and awarded a DFC. *(Peter R. Caygill)*

A Spitfire Mk VC of the 307th Fighter Squadron, 31st Fighter Group, USAAF at Ponte Olivio, Sicily in 1943. USAAF Spitfires in the Mediterranean theatre wore standard RAF desert camouflage of Dark Earth and Middle Stone. *(Philip Jarrett)*

as decoys for their comrades at a higher level. Kingaby looked up, saw the 109s above, and considered that he had just enough time to take a quick shot at the pair before the others could intervene. Having done so and zoomed back up to the protection of his section, he was surprised to be informed that he had accounted for both aircraft as they had taken evasive action and collided with each other. By the end of his tour in October, Kingaby's score was 16 plus two shared, for which he received the DFM and two Bars, becoming the only pilot to be so honoured.

Aces galore

At Hawkinge, Flight Lieutenant Jean Demozay of No. 91 Squadron was also making a name for himself. Already an ace on Hurricanes, he quickly added to his score and on 31 July 1941 managed to shoot down two Bf 109Es and damage a third out of a *Schwarm* of four. He survived the war with a total of 18 victories (13 on Spitfires) but was killed in a flying accident in 1945. Pilot Officer Keith 'Bluey' Truscott of No. 452 Squadron was a compatriot of Paddy Finucane and despite being fresh out of an Operational Training Unit (OTU) – his first

operation was on 8 July 1941 – ended the year with 11 aircraft destroyed. By the end of September he was already a hero in his native Australia, having shot down four Bf 109Fs in three days, the first during Circus 99 to Rouen on the 18th. Two days later another Circus provided Truscott with the opportunity to dispatch two more 109s, one diving into the ground after being hit in the fuselage at point-blank range and the other going into the sea. The sequence was completed on the 21st, when he shot down a fourth 109 south-west of Le Touquet. Truscott flew with No. 452 Squadron until March 1942 when he was posted to Australia to join No. 76 (RAAF) Squadron on Curtiss P-40 Kittyhawks. He was killed on 28 March 1943 when he flew into the sea while escorting a Consolidated Catalina flying-boat.

The fight for Malta

While the offensive over northern France was continued in 1942, Spitfires were also heavily involved in the battle to save Malta. Up to March 1942 only Hurricanes had been available on the island, but on the 7th the first 15 Spitfire Mk VBs were flown off the deck of HMS *Eagle* during Operation *Spotter* to provide a much-needed boost to the defences. Malta was vitally important as a naval base and as a launching pad for air operations against Axis shipping supporting German forces in North Africa. In

Spitfire VB (trop) BR390 first flew on 12 May 1942 and was carried on the *Nigerstown* to West Africa for delivery to Egypt via the Takoradi route. It is seen here in the markings of No. 145 Squadron at El Kabrit. It was damaged in a flying accident on 29 September 1942.

many ways the air war over Malta was similar to that in 1940 during the Battle of Britain, and it produced some of the most vicious fighting of the war. The most successful Malta-based pilot was Sergeant George 'Buzz' Beurling, an unpredictable Canadian who was anything but a 'team player'. Beurling had initial success with No. 41 Squadron over France, but it was felt that his lack of discipline in the air put his fellow pilots at risk and he was packed off to join No. 249 Squadron in June 1942. Very much a loner, the fighting over Malta suited his style and his score began to rise rapidly, his first combat successes occurring on 2 July when he shot down an MC.202 and a Re.2001.

By the end of July his score was already 16 destroyed, for which he received a DFM and Bar. Ordered to accept a commission in August, his score merely 'ticked over' until October when the Germans and Italians launched their last major effort to break Malta's defences. In that month Beurling claimed another eight kills, including a Ju 88 and two Bf 109Fs on consecutive days (13/14 October), but during the last combat his Spitfire Mk VC (BR173) was hit, shell splinters wounding him in the heel and forcing him to bale out. He was picked up by a rescue launch and was flown out tour-expired shortly after. His final score was 29 destroyed

plus one shared and he was also the recipient of a DFC and DSO. He went on to notch up two more victories on Spitfire Mk IXs before returning to Canada in 1944.

Another high scorer, Sergeant A.P. 'Tim' Goldsmith from Waverley, New South Wales, had been flown out in a Short Sunderland flying-boat in February, along with a number of other replacement pilots including future No. 249 Squadron aces Flying Officer Raoul Daddo-Langlois (five Malta victories), Flying Officer G.A.F. Buchanon (six) and Pilot Officer R.W. 'Buck' McNair (seven). At first Goldsmith flew Hurricanes but was soon posted to No. 126 Squadron to fly Spitfires and claimed his first victim on 21 April when he shot down a Bf 109F, most probably that of *Oberfeldwebel* Franz Kaiser of I./JG 53. On 10 May he shot down three Bf 109Fs during two sorties and followed this with a Ju 88 and another Bf 109F on the 14th. Towards the end of the month it was the turn of the Italians, Goldsmith claiming a Z.1007 bomber shot down on the 25th, although this was probably a misidentification of a Savoia-Marchetti S.M.84. Having been promoted to Pilot Officer, Goldsmith was awarded a DFC in June but he returned to the UK in July, credited with 12 victories. (In 1943 he flew Spitfire Mk VCs and shot down four

Japanese aircraft operating out of Darwin with No. 452 Squadron).

The second-highest-scoring No. 249 Squadron pilot (after Beurling) was Sergeant Ray Hesselyn from Invercargill, New Zealand. Hesselyn was another to have flown one of the initial batch of Spitfires to Malta on 7 March and although his tour only lasted to mid-July, he claimed 12 victories and received a DFM and Bar, and a DFC following his commission in May. His last Malta victories occurred on 8 July when he shot a Bf 109F into the sea during a morning raid and then set the engine of a Ju 88 alight during another attack on Luqa in the afternoon. (Hesselyn became a flight commander with No. 222 Squadron in 1943 and recorded another six kills on Spitfire Mk IXs).

Other high-scoring pilots of the Malta campaign included Flight Lieutenant Bill Rolls, who claimed nine victories with No. 126 Squadron (to add to the seven he had achieved with No. 72 Squadron in the Battle of Britain), Flight Lieutenant Wally McLeod from Regina in Saskatchewan, who quickly amassed 13 kills with Nos 603 and 1435 Squadrons, and Rhodesian Flight Lieutenant Johnny Plagis, another No. 249 Squadron pilot, with ten victories. Top-scoring No. 185 Squadron pilot was Flight Sergeant Jack 'Slim' Yarra from Queensland, who was credited with 12 aircraft shot down, a score equalled by Flight Sergeant Paddy Schade of No. 126 Squadron. Having flown with No. 41 Squadron during its successful operation from Catterick on 15 August 1940, Tony Lovell was now commander of No. 1435 Squadron and scored four kills plus two shared over Malta to add to the nine aircraft he had claimed (with another four shared) during the Battle of Britain. This made him the 11th-highest-scoring ace on early-mark Spitfires. Although he survived the war he was killed performing a slow roll shortly after take-off on 17 August 1945.

This view of a No. 64 Squadron Spitfire LF.Mk VB is one of the few to show the 'invasion' stripes worn on the outer wings of tactical fighters at the time of Operation *Starkey*, in September 1943. This was a large-scale deception timed to coincide with landings in Italy, the intention being to make the Germans think an invasion of northern France was to take place .simultaneously. *(Tony Cooper via author)*

North African aces

With the Spitfire Mk V being phased out in the west in favour of the Mk IX, one of the last opportunities for combat glory lay in North Africa. Spitfires had arrived in theatre only a matter of weeks after the first of the type to be deployed to Malta but initially were available only in very small numbers. No. 145 Squadron arrived from the UK in April 1942, becoming operational two months later, and was followed by Nos 92 and 601 Squadrons.

Several pilots ran up high scores, including Flying Officer John Taylor of No. 145 Squadron, for whom the desert campaign was to be his combat debut. His first success was a Bf 109F shot down on 8 July and over the next year he amassed 13 victories, plus two shared, before being killed in a crash-landing after his No. 601 Squadron Spitfire Mk VC (EP966) was hit by return fire from a Junkers Ju 87 near Syracuse. Wing Commander George 'Sheep' Gilroy, leader of No. 324 Wing in Tunisia, had previously commanded No. 609 Squadron at Biggin Hill in late 1941. By the time he arrived in North Africa in November 1942 he was credited with seven kills, plus another seven shared. He survived baling out on 28 January 1943 after a mid-air collision and continued to lead the Wing until November 1943, by which time it was operating over southern Italy. During this time he increased his score to 14 with another ten shared.

One of the units that comprised No. 324 Wing was No. 243 Squadron, which was joined in early 1943 by Flying Officer Evan 'Rosie' Mackie from Otorohanga, New Zealand. Mackie had previously flown with No. 485 Squadron over northern France but had only scored a half share

Above: A Spitfire Mk VC JK446, probably of No. 249 Squadron, has bomb racks under the wings and is seen at Brindisi in Italy in late 1943. *(Philip Jarrett)*

Left: Spitfire Mk VB (trop) ER810 *Inca*, served on Malta before being one of a batch of Spitfires sold to Turkey in December 1944. *(Philip Jarrett)*

in a Bf 109E before arriving in the Middle East. The change of climate, however, appeared to work, and the first of his many claims was for two Ju 87s shot down on 7 April. Later in the month he was made a flight commander but was shot down on the 24th, arriving back at base the following day with the Mk IX exhaust stubs that had been fitted to his Mk VC. Command of the squadron and a DFC were to follow and to celebrate he shot down another five aircraft in July, including two more Stukas, although on this occasion they were Italian Ju 87Rs of 121° *Gruppo*. Mackie later fought above Anzio and was given command of No. 92 Squadron (Spitfire Mk VIII) in November, his final score on Mk VCs being 12 with one shared.

Aussie aces

In early 1942 Japanese air attacks around Darwin in northern Australia prompted a request for

Spitfire Mk VCs to bolster the defences, and three squadrons (Nos 54, 452 and 457) were withdrawn from the UK to form No. 1 RAAF Fighter Wing. This did not become operational until nearly a year later, however, and the first action took place on 6 February 1943, when Flight Lieutenant Bob Foster of No. 54 Squadron shot down a Ki-46 'Dinah' on a reconnaissance mission. Japanese bombing attacks were a regular, if not constant threat over the coming months and several pilots were to achieve 'ace' status, including the aforementioned Foster. Squadron Leader Eric Gibbs of No. 54 Squadron claimed five destroyed plus one shared but was out-scored by his Wing Leader, Wing Commander Clive Caldwell, who put in claims for eight aircraft to add to the 19 he had accumulated flying P-40 Tomahawks in North Africa with Nos 250 and 112 Squadrons. Due to reversals in the Pacific, the Japanese threat to northern Australia began to wane from September and the last attack was a night raid carried out on 11/12 November 1943. No. 1 Fighter Wing's Mk VCs were replaced by Spitfire Mk VIIIs in early 1944.

4. Accomplishments

Most fighter aircraft derive their fame from success in combat and the Spitfire is no exception. Of course, to achieve such a situation an aircraft must be superior to the opposition (or have an advantage in at least one aspect of its performance) otherwise its pilots, however well trained, are unlikely to survive for very long and legendary status would quickly be replaced by something rather more derogatory. That the Spitfire was to remain at the forefront of piston-engined fighter technology from its inception to the dawn of the jet age, is testimony not only to the genius of R.J. Mitchell but to the skill of Joe Smith and his team at Supermarine who developed the basic airframe so that it would be more than a match for subsequent designs.

A snowy scene at Drem in the winter of 1939/40, as a Spitfire Mk I of No. 609 (West Riding) Squadron is run up. No. 609 stayed in Scotland until May 1940, before moving to Northolt and then to Middle Wallop during the Battle of Britain. *(Eric Watson via author)*

Above: This ex-Turkish air force Spitfire Mk I, carrying the impressment serial HK856, was photographed at El Ballah in Egypt mid-1942. As only two Spitfire Mk Is were exported to Turkey, this would appear to be either P9566 or P9567. *(Neville Duke via author)*

Cockpit view of Spitfire LF.Mk VC AR501, now with the Shuttleworth Collection. The basic flying panel instruments (top to bottom, left to right) are airspeed indicator, artificial horizon, vertical speed indicator, altimeter, direction indicator and turn and slip indicator. To the right are the engine gauges (top to bottom, left to right) rpm, fuel pressure warning lamp, boost pressure, oil pressure, oil temperature, radiator temperature and fuel contents. Between the rudder pedals is the P2 compass. *(Philip Jarrett)*

Before discussing the characteristics that made the Spitfire so special from the pilots' point of view, it is necessary to look at the reasons why the aircraft won over the hearts and minds of a generation, and has continued to be revered ever since. A brief conversation with a young boy not so long ago brought the encouraging news that he was interested in aircraft. I asked him if he had a favourite and, without having to think, he announced: 'Spitfire!' (Apparently modern aircraft, as well as failing to register on radar screens, also make very little impact on the imaginations of 10-year olds!). This situation has existed since the Spitfire was first seen on pre-war newsreels, despite the fact that the Hurricane flew first (1935), was in service first (1937), covered the 327 miles from Turnhouse to Northolt in 48 minutes (albeit with a hefty tailwind), had only marginally inferior performance, was powered by the same Rolls-Royce Merlin engine and was to shoot down more aircraft in the Battle of Britain than all other forms of defence put together. Unfortunately all of this did not count for much with the public, who continued to dream about Spitfires.

Undoubtedly, one of the main factors in the adoration of the Spitfire was the fact that it came from the same stable as the floatplane racers that had captured the Schneider Trophy outright for Britain in 1931. Huge crowds had flocked to the south coast to see the contest and the rest of the country had followed events on the cinema screen and in newspapers. The speeds achieved captured the public's imagination in what was already a very air-minded age, and the Spitfire thus had a head start to its publicity campaign. Having got the attention, its grace of line allowed it to go straight to people's hearts in a way that the Hurricane, which looked like an overweight Fury with the top wing missing, never could. Even today the Spitfire can bring a tear to the eye, when the symphony of its Merlin engine is

Spitfire Mk IIA P7490 *City of Coventry I*, of No. 66 Squadron, shows the small blister behind the spinner that housed gearing for the engine start mechanism. This aircraft later served with Nos 609, 65, 122 and 154 Squadrons, before being converted as an ASR.Mk IIC. It joined No. 277 Squadron on 9 January 1943 and was SOC on 2 June 1944. *(Philip Jarrett)*

Spitfire Mk IIA P7666 *Observer Corps* of No. 54 Squadron. It carries the two swastikas of its previous owner, Squadron Leader Don Finlay of No. 41 Squadron, which represent the two Bf 109Es he shot down on 23 and 27 November 1940. The first of these was flown by *Obergefreiter* Gunter Loppach of II./JG 51, who survived to become a PoW. JG 51 repaid the compliment on 20 April 1941, Pilot Officer Jack Stokoe baling out of P7666 over the Channel shortly after destroying a Bf 110. *(Philip Jarrett)*

L1004 had an extremely varied life. Built as a Mk I, it flew with No. 602 Squadron and No. 58 OTU, but was then converted by Scottish Aviation to Mk VA standard. After further use by No. 57 OTU, it was modified as the second prototype PR.Mk XIII, as seen here. *(Philip Jarrett)*

accompanied by the sight of an elliptical wing set against a perfect blue sky.

Another factor that was in the Spitfire's favour was its name. It was short, to the point, and seemed to sum up the mood of the nation in the increasingly troubled times of the late 1930s. It has to be said that it was not favoured by Mitchell and at one point the aircraft may have ended up being called the Shrew. If it had been, the whole Spitfire/Hurricane relationship might have been very different. Fortunately the name Shrew was quickly discarded and the way was clear for the Spitfire to ascend to its rightful place.

AA873 *Manchester Air Cadet* was the first production Spitfire Mk VC and spent most of its life on engine-related trials work. It was converted as an F.Mk IX (Merlin 61), and was later fitted with a Merlin 66 and used by de Havilland for trials with contra-rotating propellers. *(Philip Jarrett)*

Looking rather worn, Spitfire Mk VC AB488 was used solely on trials work, including the determination of propeller power coefficients at Boscombe Down in 1943, and the testing of strengthened flaps for use as air brakes, at Farnborough. It eventually became a ground instructional airframe with No. 1 School of Technical Training (SoTT) in October 1943. *(Philip Jarrett)*

Already blessed with an aura of glamour, the exigencies of war boosted the Spitfire's reputation to almost mythical proportions. The mixture of fact and fiction which enhanced its stature have been the source of constant debate ever since. When it came to providing money for the war effort, 'Spitfire Funds' began to appear in ever-increasing number, and eventually the Ministry of Aircraft Production became concerned at the public's over-identification with Mitchell's creation. In an attempt to even things up a little, any individual or organisation failing to specify what sort of fighter they wanted to sponsor, had their name or inscription applied to a Hurricane. Such bureaucratic manoeuvring failed to make much difference, however, and the vast majority of 'presentation' fighters in World War Two were Spitfires.

Just as the Spitfire was venerated by the public, it quickly came to be loved by the pilots who flew it. Its performance, fine handling qualities and almost complete lack of vices combined to leave a lasting impression. The first service pilots to fly the Spitfire were the test pilots at the Aeroplane and Armament Experimental Establishment (A&AEE), Martlesham Heath, who reported on the prototype in September 1936. Their comments as regards controllability and general handling were as follows:

'Ailerons: On the ground the aileron control works freely and without play. Full movement of the control column can be obtained when the pilot is in the cockpit. In the air the ailerons are light to handle when climbing and on the glide they become heavier with increase in speed, but by no more than is required to impart good 'feel'. The aeroplane was dived to 380 mph ASI and up to that speed the ailerons were not unduly heavy and gave adequate response. The ailerons are effective down to the stall and give adequate control when landing and taking off. The response is quick under all conditions of flight and during all manoeuvres required from a fighting aeroplane. There is no snatch or aileron vibration at any speed and in general the aileron control is excellent for a high-speed fighting aeroplane.

'Rudder: On the ground the rudder control operates freely and without play. There is an excellent adjustment for the position of the rudder bar. In the air it is moderately light and extremely effective. The rudder becomes heavier with increase of speed but by no more than is necessary in a high-speed aeroplane, and at the highest speed it is still effective. The aeroplane responds easily and quickly to rudder under all conditions of flight. Although the rudder is heavier than the ailerons, it should not be made

BR202 was the first Spitfire Mk VC to carry the 170-Imp gal slipper tank, the lack of ground clearance being evident in this view. With a further 29-Imp gal tank in the fuselage behind the pilot's seat, total fuel load was 284 Imp gal. Trials carried out at Boscombe Down in August 1942 showed range to be 1,625 miles at 15,000 ft. Take-off distance was 580 yards. *(Philip Jarrett)*

lighter as with a very light rudder the pilot might overload the aeroplane at high speed.

'Elevators: On the ground full movement of the elevators can be obtained. Operation is light and there is no play. In the air the elevator control is very light and very effective down to the stall. Heaviness increases with speed, but by no more than necessary. In the dive the aeroplane is steady. The elevators give rapid response with a small movement of the control column. When landing the control column need not be fully back. The control is satisfactory as regards 'feel' and response, but would be improved if the movement of the control column for a given movement of the elevators was slightly larger. A small movement of the control column produces so large an effect that an unskilled pilot might pull the nose of the aeroplane up too much when landing, however a change to alter the gearing between control column and elevator is not considered advisable until spinning trials show it to be safe.

'Characteristics at the stall: As the elevator control is very powerful the aeroplane will stall long before the control column is moved right back. The stall is normal. There is no vice nor snatch on the controls. In tight turns giving approximately 3*g* as registered on the accelerometer, at speeds from 140 mph ASI downwards, there was a distinct juddering of the whole aeroplane. Under these conditions the aeroplane is probably in a semi-stalled condition and this juddering effect may be due to slight

A USAAF Spitfire Mk VB carries out a low-level beat up. Spitfires were used by the 4th Fighter Group, 8th Air Force until replaced by P-47s in March 1943, and by the 31st and 52nd Fighter Groups, initially with the 8th but latterly with the 12th Air Force, until replaced by P-51s in April/May 1944. *(Peter R. Caygill)*

buffeting on the tail. This can be stopped at once if the control column is eased forward.

'Aerobatics: Loops, half-rolls off loops, slow rolls and stall turns have been done. The aeroplane is very easy and pleasant to handle in all aerobatics.

'Landing and taking-off: The aeroplane is easy and normal to take-off. There is a slight tendency to swing, but this is not so pronounced as on a Fury and is automatically and easily corrected by the pilot. The aeroplane is simple and easy to land, but requires very little movement of the control column as the elevator control is so powerful and it is not necessary to have the control column fully back. If the engine is opened up with the flaps and undercarriage down, the aeroplane can be easily held by the control column. The aeroplane does not swing on landing.

'Sideslipping: The aeroplane does not sideslip readily.

'Ground handling: The ground handling is

Spitfire LF.Mk VB BL680 was flown by No. 616 Squadron, before being handed over to the USAAF in November 1943. *(Philip Jarrett)*

exceptionally good. The aeroplane is easy to turn and taxi in fairly strong winds. It is a more satisfactory aeroplane for operating in high winds than the normal biplane fighter.'

One of the reasons for the Spitfire's controllability at low speed was that Mitchell had incorporated washout into the wing, whereby the angle of incidence at the tip was 2° less than at the root. This allowed aileron control at very low speeds as the wing stalled from root to tip, and the progressive aerodynamic buffet experienced as speed was reduced gave pilots ample warning that a stall was imminent. Stall speed with flaps and undercarriage up was 64 mph IAS, reducing to 58 mph IAS with flaps and undercarriage down. Spinning and diving trials were carried out at the A&AEE in October 1938 using K9787 with three different loadings:

1) Typical service load, weight 5,784 lb centre-of-gravity (cg) 7.8 in, aft of datum
2) Weight 5,796 lb extended aft, cg 8.7 in, aft of datum
3) Weight 5,338 lb forward, cg 6.0 in, aft of datum

The limiting position for cg was found to be

6.0 in to 8.7 in, aft of datum corresponding to 0.32–0.35 aerodynamic mean chord.

Test results were as follows:

'Spins from straight stalls: The aeroplane is easy to spin but the first three turns are uneven, especially when spinning to the right when there is a pronounced variation of rotational speed during each turn, the nose rising and falling and large changes of sideslip occurring. After the first three turns the spin becomes smooth and steady except to the right at loading (b) when the spin is rough throughout. The spin appears to be flatter at the aftmost position of the cg. Much buffeting and vibration is felt during the first three turns though this is not so noticeable at the forward position of cg. In spins to the right at aft cg position, the rudder and ailerons snatch slightly.

'Spins from stalled turns: In entering the spin from stalled turns the aeroplane makes a most violent series of evolutions before settling down into a steady spin after two or three turns. It pitches violently and feels as if it might turn on

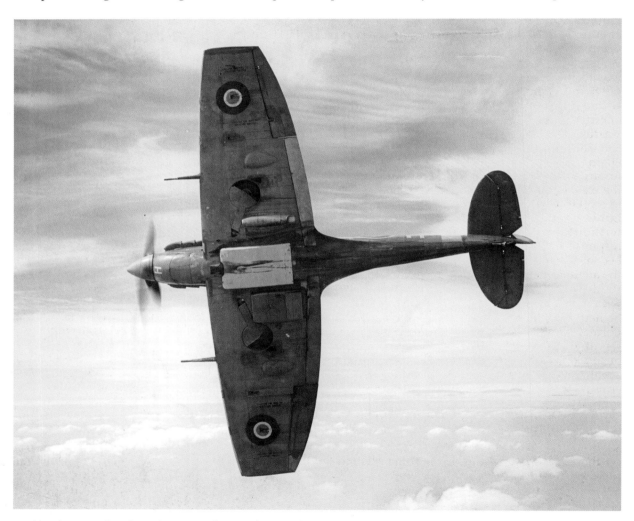

Underside view of a clipped-wing Spitfire LF.Mk VB with a 30-Imp gal slipper tank. Removal of the wing tips greatly improved roll response and in comparative trials with a standard aircraft at the AFDU at Duxford, the latter was unable to follow a clipped-wing Mk V, which could quickly get on the tail of the unmodified machine. *(Philip Jarrett)*

its back and the pilot is thrown about the cockpit.

'Spins from gliding turns: From a gentle gliding turn the aeroplane falls into the spin without violent manoeuvres.

'Spins with stick forward: At the forward limit during one spin the stick was put forward after the first turn. This had the result of speeding up the rate of rotation very considerably and the spin became flatter.

'Recovery: Using full opposite rudder and moving the control column gently forward after full rudder has been applied is the best recovery method, and with this method the recovery is easy in 1–2 turns. When rotation ceases the aeroplane is in a semi-stalled condition and there is a strong tendency to flick into another spin in either direction.

'Diving: The aeroplane is steady in the dive with engine running correctly but some pitching occurs when the engine cuts in and out. Vibration is experienced at speeds between 350–380 mph ASI and above 400 mph ASI the engine cuts in and out. This may easily give rise to large accelerations owing to the lightness of the elevator control and would be disconcerting to a relatively inexperienced pilot. Slight control movements were made at maximum speed without control instability resulting and response to the controls is normal. All controls become heavier especially ailerons and rudder, the ailerons becoming almost immovable and the rudder extremely heavy. Tail heaviness develops with increase of speed and the aeroplane has to be held into the dive; this is most marked at the normal cg when the force required to hold into the dive is very considerable. Recovery is easy but care must be taken not to apply excessive accelerations as the control column tends to come back strongly [apart from lack of manoeuvrability, problems were also experienced with the hood, which could not be opened in dives at more than 300 mph ASI, prompting the development of a breakout panel on the port side of the canopy to equalise the pressure inside and outside the cockpit]'.

Spitfire Mk VC BR166 was first flown on 7 March 1942, before being dispatched to Malta, where it joined No. 185 Squadron and was coded 'GL-A'. It survived until 19 September 1944, when it was lost on operations. *(Philip Jarrett)*

Spitfire Mk VC EE627 was flown by Nos 602 and 29 Squadrons in late 1942, but was involved in a flying accident on 23 January 1943. After repair it was used by Nos 52, 57 and 61 OTUs and was SOC on 5 June 1945. *(Philip Jarrett)*

A further series of trials was carried out by A&AEE in June 1939, again using K9787. As regards stability, the aircraft was generally stable at all speeds, although it tended to be unstable longitudinally when cg was moved aft of the normal position. With flaps and undercarriage up, turns could be made down to 70 mph IAS in either direction and recovery could be made with either rudder or aileron held fixed. With the control column right back, the aircraft could be held in a straight path only for a few seconds by the careful use of rudder and ailerons. It then pitched and tried to go into a diving turn in either direction but this could be checked by use of rudder when a 'falling leaf' resulted. There was no tendency to spin. With gear and flaps down, turns could be made down to 60 mph IAS in either direction.

For landing the best approach speed was 85 mph IAS and, once again, care had to be

Known by the press as the '109 specialist', Flight Sergeant Don Kingaby of No. 92 Squadron was one of the RAF's top Spitfire scorers and was the only NCO pilot to be awarded three DFMs. He went on to command the Hornchurch Wing in mid-1943, and ended the war at the Advanced Gunnery School at Catfoss. His final victory tally amounted to 21 aircraft destroyed, with another two shared. *(Peter R. Caygill)*

taken not to overdo things with the powerful elevator control. In a go-around situation, with flaps and undercarriage down, the aircraft became tail heavy and although this could be held until re-trimmed, the resultant climb away was poor. As the deflection angle of the flaps had been increased from the prototype's 57° to a full 90°, general handling qualities during final approach were improved considerably. Later in the year the first Spitfire to be equipped with Hispano cannon (L1007) was tested at the A&AEE, when the following performance measurements were taken:

Aircraft	K9787	K9793	L1007
Airscrew	2 blade wood	DH Type, two pitch, three blade	DH Type, two pitch, three blade
Engine	Merlin II	Merlin II	Merlin III
Time to 20,000 ft	9 minutes 24 seconds	11 minutes 24 seconds	10 minutes 42 seconds
Speed at 18,500 ft	363 mph	367 mph	364 mph
Service ceiling	31,900 ft	34,400 ft	34,500 ft

Handling qualities of the cannon-armed Spitfire were the same as for aircraft equipped with machine-guns, and the only reduction in performance was a drop in top speed of 3 mph caused by increased drag.

The main adversary of the Spitfire Mk I was the Messerschmitt Bf 109E and although on paper it had similar performance, in the air it was different in a number of ways. In comparison with the Spitfire, the 109 had a better rate of climb and was able to climb at a particularly steep angle when full throttle was selected at low airspeed. Being fitted with a Daimler-Benz DB 601A with fuel injection, it was also able to carry out a bunt manoeuvre without the engine cutting out, as it did on the carburettor-equipped Merlin. The 109 also had excellent control at low speeds and the stall was

gentle even when pulling g in a turn. It was also a good high-altitude fighter, and generally out-performed the Spitfire above 20,000 ft.

In many other respects however, the Spitfire was the better of the two. When it came to control harmony, a contemporary RAF report on a captured Bf 109E considered that 'harmony' was a somewhat inappropriate word to describe the control forces experienced during high-speed flight. Like the Spitfire, the 109's ailerons became progressively heavier at speeds above 300 mph, but so too did its elevators, which severely restricted manoeuvrability. In some cases Spitfire pilots were able to tempt their counterparts into a half-roll and dive at low level, knowing that the 109 was unlikely to pull out before hitting the ground. The pilot of a 109 had great difficulty in pulling enough g to black himself out as stick force per g was in the order of 20 lb. The rudder was the lightest of the controls on the 109, but as there was no cockpit trimmer the pilot had to apply considerable effort to keep the aircraft pointing in the right direction.

The Spitfire was clearly superior in the turn, but only if it was flown to its limit. This was due to lower wing loading (25 lb/sq ft as opposed to 32 lb/sq ft on the 109), but the latter's benign stalling characteristics at least gave its pilots the confidence to pull hard into a turn, and some Spitfires were out-turned by 109s when pilots of the former did not extract the aircraft's full performance. In a turning fight the 109 also suffered due to its lack of rudder trim and occasional asymmetric operation of the leading edge slats, which were liable to cause the nose to wander at inappropriate moments. In an ideal world, RAF pilots would have generally preferred to fight in the horizontal plane, while their opponents would have liked to have used the 109's excellent vertical penetration as much as possible. In the real world, however, the pilot who saw the other first usually came out on top.

At the other end of the speed range, a trial was carried out in April 1940 under the auspices of the Air Fighting Development Unit (AFDU), using a Lysander and a section of Spitfire Mk Is from No. 65 Squadron. This was primarily intended to formulate tactics for army co-operation crews, who were likely to encounter single-engined fighters over France. For the Lysander, early warning of an attack was essential, but assuming that the Spitfire was seen in good time the chances of survival were surprisingly high. The best evasive technique was to fly a steep spiral descent at maximum angle of bank using the engine to increase the

rate of turn if the Spitfire got within firing range. If this could be maintained down to ground level, the Lysander could then use ground cover to escape. Spitfire pilots found it extremely difficult to follow a steep turning descent at low speed and had to throttle back to around 90 mph IAS. If the guns had been fired at this speed the recoil forces would have knocked off another 20 mph or so, leaving the Spitfire perilously close to a stall/spin.

Although the Spitfire is rightly regarded as a classic, it was only as good as the man in the cockpit. To be successful he had to be able to utilise the Spitfire's potential to the full, show high levels of tactical awareness, and at the same time display exceptional skills as a marksman. These qualities were held in abundance by Flight Sergeant Don Kingaby, DFM of No. 92 Squadron, who used them to good effect during a sweep over northern France on 1 October 1941 and a Circus operation two days later. His combat reports highlight the Spitfire at its best and the predatory nature that was needed to become an

Spitfire Mk VB W3320 *The Darlington Spitfire*, was Don Kingaby's personal aircraft from 20 July to 16 October 1941 and during this period he shot down three Bf 109Fs with another three probables. After conversion as an LF.Mk VB, W3320 claimed a half-share in a Bf 109G on 27 July 1943 when flown by Pilot Officer Roy Flight of No. 118 Squadron. It also flew with Nos 54, 64, 611, 234 and 63 Squadrons but was written off when hit by another Spitfire at North Weald on 28 October 1944, by which time it had flown 212 operational sorties. *(Peter R. Caygill)*

One of No. 601 Squadron's Spitfire Mk VCs (EP455). This aircraft lasted operationally for less than a month and was abandoned on 2 November 1942 shortly after the launching of the El Alamein offensive. *(Philip Jarrett)*

ace: 'I took off with Garrick squadron (No. 92) as BLUE 1 at 11:30 hrs for a Channel sweep. I led BLUE 2 after four aircraft which I thought were 109s going towards Gris Nez just below the cloud base at 13,000 ft, but we were unable to catch them up. We were then jumped by four 109s which dived out of the cloud and I had to pull up into it as evasive action. BLUE 2 became detached. I waited underneath the cloud base until I saw four 109s approaching from inland on my front port quarter about half a mile away. I pulled up into cloud and turned to the left, came down again and found the 109s pitching into a gaggle of Spitfires. I attacked one 109 which showed me his belly in plan view at about 40–50-yards range. I gave him a one-second burst of cannon and machine-gun and he went down with glycol pouring from both radiators.

'I then flew inland over France about ten miles, still keeping just below cloud base, and resorted to the same trick when I saw a gaggle of eight 109s coming towards me on my front port quarter. This time I came out of the cloud about 50 yards to the right and 100 yards behind them. I chose the last 109 and opened fire in a quarter, turning to a stern attack, giving a four-second burst. Pieces fell from him, his glycol was hit and then the enemy aircraft just fell away in a dive, breaking up into separate parts as it did so. The tail parted company with the aircraft. I took a squirt at another 109 with machine-gun only but had to beat it into the cloud owing to the persistence of the other 109s. Flew back in cloud and landed at Gravesend.'

On 3 October 1941 Kingaby flew as No. 92 Squadron's YELLOW 3 in Circus 105, an attack by six Blenheims of No. 88 Squadron on a power station at Ostend. Due to losses the previous day, No. 92 could only put up two sections of four aircraft: 'Garrick squadron took off from Biggin Hill at 13:38 hrs on Circus 105 as escort cover. We rendezvoused with the bombers and escort over Clacton and proceeded to the target at Ostend. There was a fair amount of flak over the target and one large fire started by the bombers. My R/T and reflector sight died over the target due to an electrical fault. Shortly after leaving the target I saw eight 109s behind the squadron with another 12 supporting them, all about 300 yards away. I could not warn the squadron as my R/T was dead, so I turned round into them. The 109s were very quick and without diving to accelerate they closed on my No. 4 and shot him down at 50-yards range [No. 92 Squadron in fact lost two pilots – Sergeants H. Cox (W3710) and G.E.F. Woods-Scawen (AB779)]. I mixed it with about six of them, but my cockpit was suddenly flooded with glycol and I thought I had been badly hit. I decided to try and draw off the 109s from the squadron and head for the English coast before the engine failed. I went into a snaking dive at full throttle with three 109s firing at me and another four behind. The manoeuvre succeeded in saving the rest of the squadron from being bounced. One 109 did not give up the chase and overhauled me.

Carrying the marking *Malta's 1,000th* under the windscreen, this Mk VC (EP829) flew with No. 249 Squadron and was one of a batch of 19 Spitfire Mk Vs transferred to the Italian air force on 27 June 1946. It became MM4069. *(Philip Jarrett)*

'I went into a steep turn to the left with the 109 firing a deflection shot at 150 yards. After two turns I began to out-turn him and the 109 broke off and pulled up above me, half-rolled, changed his mind again and rolled back heading for France. By this time I had got on his tail at about 100-yards range at 1,000 ft. I chased him down to 500 ft giving him a two-to-three-second burst of cannon and machine-gun. As the reflector sight was u/s [unserviceable] I had had a bead sight fitted and I used this. My burst caused a big puff of black smoke to issue from the enemy aircraft and he dived straight into the Channel. I proceeded to Manston and found that I had not collected a single bullet. The glycol in the cockpit had come from the glycol tank in the windscreen anti-freeze device which had gone wrong.'

The machine Kingaby used on both of these sorties was Spitfire Mk VB W3320 *The Darlington Spitfire*, which was his personal aircraft for the last three months of his tour with No. 92 Squadron. W3320 went on to fly over 200 operational sorties with seven squadrons before being damaged beyond repair when hit by another Spitfire at North Weald in October 1944.

Following operational use, most early Spitfires were retired from first-line duties and issued to OTUs, where they were used to give pilots their

Spitfire Mk VC ER220 'QJ-R', of No. 92 Squadron, after a mishap. This was Flight Lieutenant Neville Duke's personal aircraft in early 1943 and it carries No. 92's 'East India Squadron' marking ahead of the victory symbols. These latter show two rows of six, comprising claims for four German and eight Italian aircraft. Duke used this machine to shoot down an MC.202 on 8 January 1943 and a Ju 87 on 21 January. *(Philip Jarrett)*

first experience of a high-speed fighter. Flight Lieutenant Tony Cooper passed through No. 61 OTU, Rednal in mid-1943, prior to a tour on No. 64 Squadron, initially flying the LF.Mk VB and later the Spitfire Mk IX. Unlike most trainees, Cooper had considerable flying experience with nearly 2,000 hours in his logbook, having been an instructor for two and a half years on Fairey Battles, and North American Yales and Harvards with No. 31 Flying Training School at Kingston, Ontario in Canada. He recalled: 'One thing I must say is that I never joined the Air Force to be an instructor! I joined because I wanted to fly Spitfires – it seemed to be a wonderful thing to be able to do at the time. Eventually, after waiting a very long time, I was able to join in and do the job that I had wanted to do when I joined the RAF in 1937.

'I first flew the Spitfire at 61 OTU at Rednal. Even though the aircraft there were second-line, the thrill of seeing a Spitfire close to and being able to sit in one and fly it was something I had dreamed about for years and years. Having been an instructor I never thought I would have the luck to be posted to a Spitfire squadron. Suddenly I was getting into an aircraft that did twice the speed of the last one I had flown, and it was one of the most thrilling moments of my life to go down that runway flat out in a Spitfire. The first thing one realised was that because of its powerful engine and the large propeller of nearly 11 ft in diameter, there was a very definite pull to the left when the tail came up, but you were ready for it and instinctively applied right rudder to keep the thing straight. Of course as soon as it reached flying speed it flew like any other aeroplane.

'After the Spitfire Is and IIs at OTU, I didn't notice a great deal of difference when I got onto the V, they were newer aeroplanes and had less paint scraped off, but they were heavier as they were fully armed and we later put extra tanks on for longer range. The Spitfire was very light on the controls, although obviously as speed increased the controls got heavier. You could almost fly it like a First World War biplane, you could sideslip it and rudder off any extra speed on landing to put her down almost one wheel at a time if you wanted to. Despite its narrow undercarriage the number of accidents that we had were few. Every aeroplane flew slightly differently, you couldn't fly

it hands off for any length of time but that wasn't really to be expected of a fighter. Although my favourite Spitfire has to be the Mark IX, I enjoyed the Mark V with the clipped wings, it was a lovely aeroplane to roll and to play around with. It was beautiful to fly and I enjoyed it very much indeed.'

Many pilots rated the clipped-wing Spitfire Mk V as the best of the lot as it retained the agility of the early Marks but had more power. Others were less complimentary although this did not reflect badly on the aircraft itself, it merely reflected the fact that performance had been surpassed by more advanced versions and by newer designs. As for being a legend, the Spitfire, perhaps more than any other World War Two fighter, is deserving of the title, and not just because of its wartime exploits. For many it was a symbol of hope and it was to play a vital role in maintaining Britain's morale when the country was fighting for its very survival in 1940. The facts do not always fit the legend, but this is of little importance. Despite the protestations of the Hurricane lobby, the Spitfire myth seems set to continue! As for its pilots, the Spitfire provided the means by which they could take the war to the enemy, and it gave them the confidence to know that if they did their job properly it would never let them down. Not only was it a consummate weapon of war, its handling qualities were such that, after 60 years, the pleasure derived from an aerobatic sortie is still fondly remembered. Happily there are still many Spitfires in airworthy condition for succeeding generations to see what all the fuss was about. For some they will be the beginning of a lifelong fascination.

Perhaps the last word should go to Flight Lieutenant Jim Pickering, who flew Spitfires with No. 64 Squadron in the Battle of Britain, with No. 145 Squadron in the Desert Air Force and also as a test pilot with No. 3501 Servicing Unit (SU) at Cranfield: 'The Spitfire has some faults – what complicated piece of equipment hasn't? If you made your pick from a line of chorus girls, it would probably be the long-legged blonde. She might on occasion put on a show of bad temper, but you would put up with it for the pleasure she contributed and the jealousy she aroused. I flew as a pilot for 61 years. If I could repeat just one flight, it would be my first solo in a Spitfire on 17 June 1940.'

5. Variants

Spitfire Mk I

Although similar in appearance to the prototype, the first production Spitfire Mk Is demonstrated a number of detail differences to K5054 in its original form. The tailskid was replaced by a castoring tailwheel, and the small hinged doors that had shielded the mainwheel tyres were deleted. Flush exhausts were replaced by triple ejector exhausts and power was provided by a 1,030-hp Merlin II in the first 174 aircraft, before being replaced by a Merlin III. The first 77 production Mk Is were fitted with the Airscrew Company's Weybridge two-bladed, fixed-pitch propeller. This was replaced from the 78th machine with a three-bladed, two-speed de Havilland propeller. By the height of the Battle of Britain, however, most of these had been replaced by constant-speed airscrews. Although these units were considerably heavier than fixed-pitch propellers, performance was improved considerably, in particular take-off distance, climb rate and service ceiling. Top speed was also increased by 4 mph.

A further increase in performance was obtained in early 1940, when 87-octane petrol was replaced by fuel rated at 100 octane. This allowed higher

This early production Spitfire Mk I, K9804, joined No. 66 Squadron on 23 October 1938, moving to No. 616 Squadron almost exactly a year later. After being damaged in a night landing, it went missing on 28 May 1940 when the squadron was operating out of Rochford. *(Philip Jarrett)*

This is a very unusual Spitfire. It appears to have the small blister on the right-hand side of the cowling indicative of a Mk II, but with an early flat-topped canopy. The 'cannon' installation could be a mock-up and the narrow-diameter propeller has quite a broad chord at the tip. The large hangar in the background and the overall lighting suggest that this photo was not taken in Britain. Over to you! *(Philip Jarrett)*

boost pressures to be used without the risk of detonation within the engine. Early Spitfire Mk Is featured a flat-topped hood, but this was soon replaced by a domed canopy for better pilot comfort. Other modifications carried out after the Spitfire had entered service included a redesigned aerial mast, the addition of a bulletproof panel to the external surface of the windscreen and armour protection behind the pilot's seat.

Armament was initially eight 0.303-in Browning machine-guns with 300 rounds per gun, the first trial fitting of two 20-mm Hispano cannon taking place in June 1939, when L1007 was converted. This aircraft had all Browning guns deleted, but due to the continued unreliability of the Hispano, cannon-armed Spitfires were later to be fitted with Brownings in the outer wing positions. The eight-gun wing was known as the 'A' wing, with the Hispano/Browning combination being referred to as the 'B' wing. This produced the revised designation of Mark IA for eight-gun aircraft and Mark IB for machines armed with cannon.

As the Spitfire was also intended for use at night, retractable landing lamps were fitted in the wings and were lowered by the aircraft's pneumatic system. Navigation and identification lamps were also fitted. Many aircraft were also fitted with 'blinker' plates on the rear of the engine cowling to shield the exhaust flame and protect the pilot's night vision. At first a single-exposure gun-camera was fitted in the leading edge of the port wing but this was soon replaced

Spitfire PR.Mk IV BP888 was fitted with a Merlin 46 and an F.24 oblique camera. Pictured during trials at Boscombe Down in May 1943, it had previously flown from Benson. BP888 was delivered to No. 8 OTU at Dyce on 10 September 1943 to train future PR pilots, but crashed on 27 October 1944. *(Philip Jarrett)*

by a G.42B cine-camera operated by the gun-firing button on the control column, although in cannon-armed aircraft activation was via the cannon-firing pipeline. Fuel was carried in two tanks between the firewall and the cockpit, the upper tank holding 48 Imp gal, and the lower tank 37 Imp gal. A 5.8-Imp gal oil tank was carried under the nose and was contoured to fit within the tightly fitting lower engine cowling. For windscreen de-icing, glycol solution was pumped from a tank mounted on the starboard side of the cockpit just above the bottom longeron and sprayed over the front screen.

Spitfire Mk Is converted as photo-reconnaissance machines generally flew without guns, radio and emergency flares, and much attention was given to external finish to increase top speed. Most were fitted with revised hoods with side blisters for extra visibility, and some

Table showing Spitfire Mk I photo-reconnaissance conversions.

long-range variants had an enlarged oil tank that required a deeper profile to the bottom engine cowling. Sub-variants are listed in the accompanying table (although the Type D and G were based on the Mk V, for completeness they have been included in this section).

Spitfire Mark II

The Spitfire Mk II was virtually identical to the Mk I apart from having a Merlin XII and Coffman cartridge (in place of electric) start. Its only external difference was a small blister behind the spinner on the right-hand side of the engine cowling covering the reduction gearing for the starter. Like the Mk I, sub-variants were the eight-gun Mk IIA and the cannon-armed Mk IIB. A number of Mk IIs were modified to carry an external fuel tank to improve range, this arrangement having been tested on a Spitfire Mk I (K9791). This involved a fixed 40-Imp gal tank mounted under the port wing, the LR version of the Spitfire Mk II being delivered to

Type	Representative serials	Fuel	Cameras	Remarks
PR.Mk IA	N3069, N3071	Standard	F.24 (5 in) in wings (later 8 in)	Pale green 'Camotint'. Perspex side blisters to canopy
PR.Mk IB	P9331	+29 Imp gal fuselage tank	F.24 (8 in) in wings	
PR.Mk IC	P9426, R6903	+29 Imp gal tank and 30 Imp gal blister tank under wing	F.24 (8 in) in starboard wing blister	R6903 had revised engine cowling for enlarged oil tank
PR.Mk ID	P9551, P9552	+29 Imp gal tank and 114 Imp gal in wing leading edges (later 133 Imp gal)	2 x F.24 (8 in or 20 in) or 2 x F.8 (20 in) in fuselage	Merlin 45, later PR.Mk IV. Extra oil tank carried in port wing. Rounded windscreen
PR.Mk IE	N3117	+29 Imp gal fuselage tank	F.24 in bulged fairing under each wing for low-level photography	Light pink colour scheme. Carried 'LY' codes of PRU
PR.Mk IF	X4502	+29 Imp gal tank and 2 x 30 Imp gal underwing blister tanks	2 x F.24 (8 in, later 20 in) in fuselage. Oblique F.24 fitted later	Enlarged oil tank
PR.Mk IG	R7059, R7116, X4784	+29 Imp gal fuselage tank	2 x F.24 (5 and 14 in) in fuselage + 1 x F.24 oblique (14 in)	Merlin 45, later PR.Mk VII. Retained guns. Most light pink though some camouflaged. Pink a/c often had roundels inboard

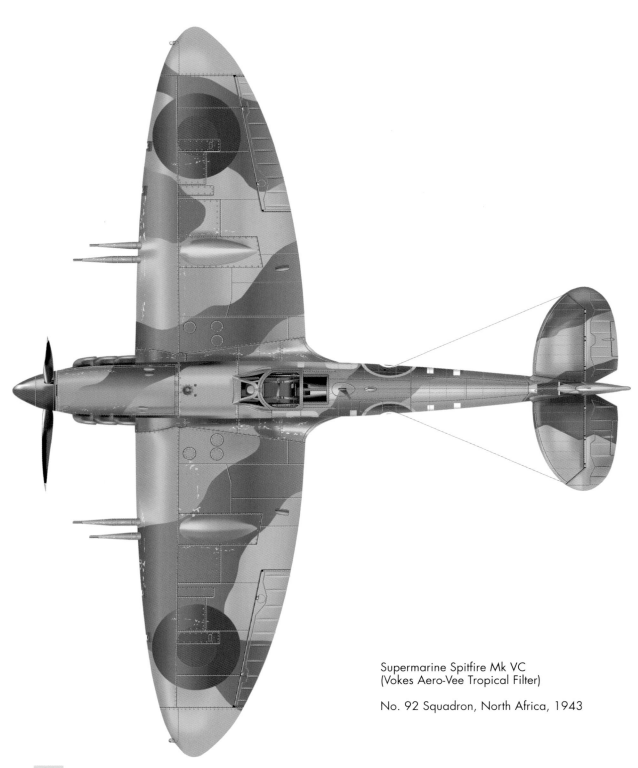

Supermarine Spitfire Mk VC
(Vokes Aero-Vee Tropical Filter)

No. 92 Squadron, North Africa, 1943

Above: This view of Spitfire PR.Mk IV R7034 shows up well the altered nose profile for the enlarged oil tank, necessary because of the aircraft's greatly increased endurance. Sorties of over five hours' duration were commonplace. Later aircraft had an 18-Imp gal oil tank fitted in the port wing. *(Philip Jarrett)*

Nos 66, 118, 152, 234 and 501 Squadrons for bomber escort work to the Brest peninsula. The weight and drag of the asymmetric installation caused handling problems and this form of overload tank was quickly discarded, although some long-range Spitfire Mk IIs were passed on to Nos 19, 222 and 616 Squadrons.

During 1942 a number of Spitfire Mk IIs were converted for use by Air-Sea Rescue (ASR) squadrons as Mk IICs, although on this occasion the 'C' had nothing to do with armament and was merely used to differentiate ASR aircraft from the fighter versions. Armament was retained, and a rack was mounted under the port

Spitfire PR.Mk IV BR419 was flown for the first time on 9 May 1942 and delivered to No. 1 PRU later that month. After Cat. B damage during operations on 2 August 1942 it was repaired, and joined No. 543 Squadron at the end of October. It ended its days with No. 8 OTU and was written off on 31 December 1943. *(Philip Jarrett)*

Below: A Spitfire Mk II (LR) of No. 66 Squadron flying low over the sea. The fixed fuel tank under the port wing cut top speed by about 30 mph and caused handling problems which were particularly noticeable during take-off and landing, and in the circuit. *(Philip Jarrett)*

wing adjacent to the oil cooler for the carriage of two smoke bombs for use as markers. The flare chutes in the fuselage were modified so that canisters containing a dinghy and food could be carried. These Spitfire Mk IIs were re-designated ASR.Mk II in late 1942, and were flown by Nos 275, 276, 277, 278 and 282 Squadrons until replaced by similar versions of the Spitfire Mk V in 1944.

Spitfire Mk III

Although the Mk III did not go into production, several of its features were incorporated into subsequent versions of the Spitfire. The wings were capable of accommodating various armament configurations up to four 20-mm Hispano cannon, and formed the basis of the Type 'C' or 'universal' wing of the Spitfire Mk VC. They were also of reduced span, with squared-off tips, which were to reappear in the clipped wings of the LF.Mk V. The Mark III also had a retractable tailwheel, which was to become standard on Griffon-engined Spitfires, more armour and had the 'bulletproof' panel of the windscreen mounted internally, a feature that was to appear on late-model LF.Mk Vs. In an attempt to reduce aerodynamic drag to a minimum, the small wheel doors of the prototype made a reappearance. Such refinements, together with the power of a 1,240-hp two-speed Rolls-Royce Merlin XX, raised top speed to 385 mph. Following the rejection of the Spitfire Mk III in favour of the Mk V, the prototype (N3297) was fitted with a Merlin 61 and was used as a development aircraft for the Spitfire Mk IX.

In addition to its many other improvements, Spitfire Mk III N3297 had its mainwheel legs splayed forward by a further 2° in an attempt to improve the Spitfire's stability when taxiing. *(Philip Jarrett)*

Spitfire Mk IV and Mk XX

The Spitfire Mk IV was the first of the Griffon-engined Spitfires and the prototype (DP845) was flown for the first time by Jeffrey Quill on 27 November 1941. It was powered by a single-stage Griffon IIB coupled to a four-bladed propeller, but unlike later Griffon-powered Spitfires, retained the circular section oil cooler of the Mk V under its port wing. In early 1942, DP845 was re-designated Mk XX to avoid confusion with the PR.Mk IV photo-reconnaissance variant and was later developed into the Mk XII, which saw limited service.

Spitfire Mk V

Although initially considered as a temporary expedient until the high-altitude Spitfire Mk VI became available, the Mk V was to be the mainstay of Fighter Command from 1941-43 until replaced by the Spitfire Mk IX. The Mk V was powered by a 1,440-hp Merlin 45 which raised full-throttle height to 19,000 ft, an improvement of 3,000 ft over the Merlin III as fitted to the Spitfire Mk I. Just as the Mk II was virtually identical to the Mk I, externally the Spitfire Mk V was little different to its immediate predecessor, a larger oil cooler under the port wing being the only major change.

Other engines that powered the Spitfire Mk V were the high-altitude Merlin 46 fitted with a larger blower of 10.85-in diameter (in place of the standard 10.25-in diameter impeller) and various derivatives of the Merlin 50 series which featured negative-g carburettors. This was an attempt to cure one of the Spitfire's most serious failings, the Merlin's inability to perform in conditions of negative-g due to fuel starvation. The new carburettor featured a diaphragm to prevent fuel being thrown to the top of the float chamber and although the theory was simple enough, it took

After the demise of the Mk III, N3297 had its Merlin XX engine replaced by a Merlin 61 and four-bladed Rotol propeller, as part of the Spitfire Mk IX development programme. The new combination gave greatly increased performance and in January 1942, during trials at Boscombe Down, N3297 achieved 414 mph at 27,000 ft. *(Philip Jarrett)*

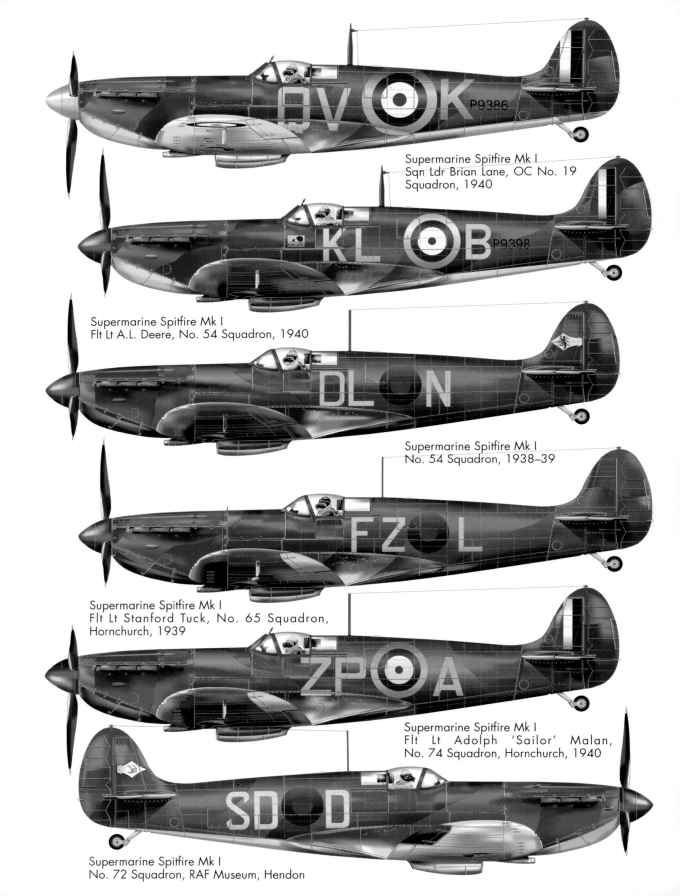

Supermarine Spitfire Mk I
Sqn Ldr Brian Lane, OC No. 19
Squadron, 1940

Supermarine Spitfire Mk I
Flt Lt A.L. Deere, No. 54 Squadron, 1940

Supermarine Spitfire Mk I
No. 54 Squadron, 1938–39

Supermarine Spitfire Mk I
Flt Lt Stanford Tuck, No. 65 Squadron,
Hornchurch, 1939

Supermarine Spitfire Mk I
Flt Lt Adolph 'Sailor' Malan,
No. 74 Squadron, Hornchurch, 1940

Supermarine Spitfire Mk I
No. 72 Squadron, RAF Museum, Hendon

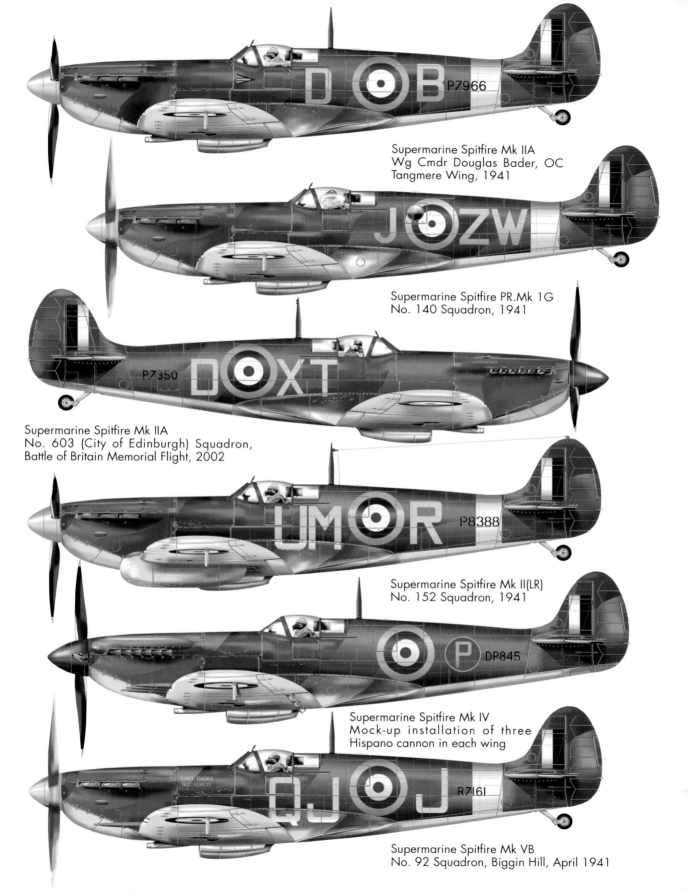

Supermarine Spitfire Mk IIA
Wg Cmdr Douglas Bader, OC
Tangmere Wing, 1941

Supermarine Spitfire PR.Mk 1G
No. 140 Squadron, 1941

Supermarine Spitfire Mk IIA
No. 603 (City of Edinburgh) Squadron,
Battle of Britain Memorial Flight, 2002

Supermarine Spitfire Mk II(LR)
No. 152 Squadron, 1941

Supermarine Spitfire Mk IV
Mock-up installation of three
Hispano cannon in each wing

Supermarine Spitfire Mk VB
No. 92 Squadron, Biggin Hill, April 1941

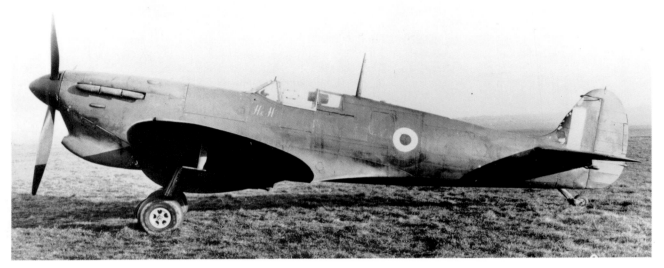

Above: Supermarine Spitfire Mk I X4922 *H & H* was converted in February 1941 as a Mk VA prototype, with a Merlin M46 engine, and is seen here in December 1941 fitted with a Vokes filter and wooden mock-up of a 90-Imp gal slipper tank. After performing trials work, it flew with No. 349 Squadron, and Nos 61 and 52 OTUs. It was SOC on 17 November 1944. *(Philip Jarrett)*

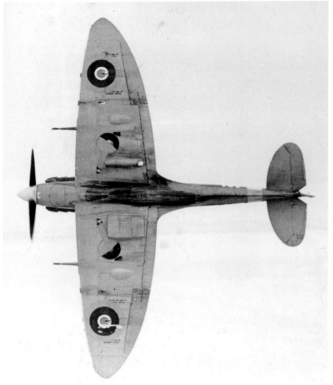

The classic lines of the Spitfire are shown to advantage in this view of Mk VB EN821 of No. 243 Squadron. *(Philip Jarrett)*

some time for the system to be perfected. The late Flight Lieutenant Dave Glaser of No. 234 Squadron once recalled to the author an occasion when he was asked to test one of the new carburettors in a Spitfire Mk VB (AD180) on 31 January 1942. Unfortunately when he applied negative-*g*, the engine coughed and died just like all the others. (Several other pilots have claimed that their aircraft must have been missed when it came to having a negative-*g* carburettor fitted!). There was, however, a benefit in using a carburettor as opposed to fuel-injection, since the evaporation of the fuel before it reached the supercharger had the effect of cooling the charge and increasing power, especially at altitude, an advantage thus denied the Bf 109 and Fw 190.

A more radical revision resulted in the M-series Merlin (45M, 50M and 55M), which featured a cropped supercharger impeller of 9.5-in diameter. This had the effect of reducing full-throttle height to 5,900 ft and was a direct response to the threat posed by the Fw 190. Maximum combat boost was raised to +18 lb/sq in and top speed was

increased to 350 mph at low altitude, a figure that was comparable to the Fw 190A and slightly better than the Bf 109G. From mid-1943 the M-series Merlin was fitted to most Spitfire Mk Vs that were likely to encounter opposition during operations. A few Spitfire Mk Vs were fitted with engines that featured the so-called 'Basta' modifications which allowed operation up to

Spitfire Mk VB (trop) shows to advantage its Vokes tropical filter and the fit of its slipper tank. It also features the much neater windscreen, with additional protective glazing mounted internally.

Spitfire LF.Mk VB EP689 'UF-X' of No. 601 Squadron, fitted with an Aboukir filter and seen at Gerbini in Sicily in 1943. *(Both Philip Jarrett)*

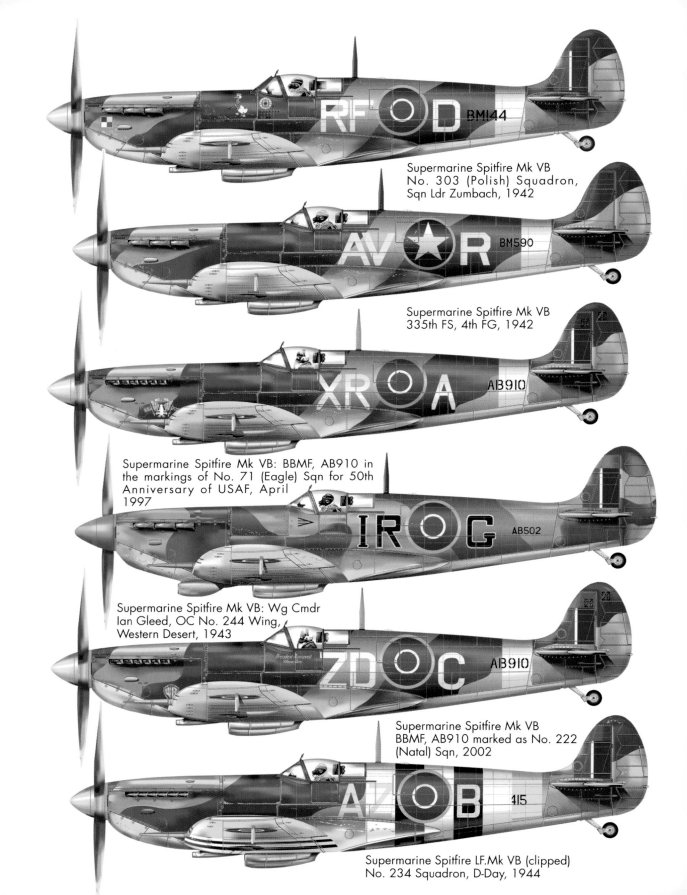

Supermarine Spitfire Mk VB
No. 303 (Polish) Squadron,
Sqn Ldr Zumbach, 1942

Supermarine Spitfire Mk VB
335th FS, 4th FG, 1942

Supermarine Spitfire Mk VB: BBMF, AB910 in
the markings of No. 71 (Eagle) Sqn for 50th
Anniversary of USAF, April
1997

Supermarine Spitfire Mk VB: Wg Cmdr
Ian Gleed, OC No. 244 Wing,
Western Desert, 1943

Supermarine Spitfire Mk VB
BBMF, AB910 marked as No. 222
(Natal) Sqn, 2002

Supermarine Spitfire LF.Mk VB (clipped)
No. 234 Squadron, D-Day, 1944

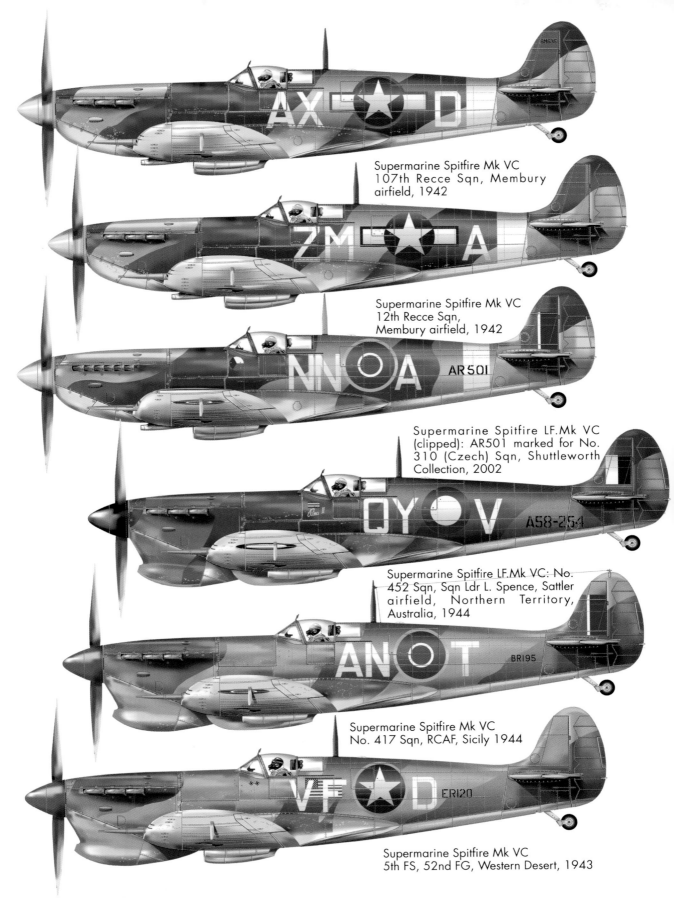

Supermarine Spitfire Mk VC
107th Recce Sqn, Membury
airfield, 1942

Supermarine Spitfire Mk VC
12th Recce Sqn,
Membury airfield, 1942

Supermarine Spitfire LF.Mk VC
(clipped): AR501 marked for No.
310 (Czech) Sqn, Shuttleworth
Collection, 2002

Supermarine Spitfire LF.Mk VC: No.
452 Sqn, Sqn Ldr L. Spence, Sattler
airfield, Northern Territory,
Australia, 1944

Supermarine Spitfire Mk VC
No. 417 Sqn, RCAF, Sicily 1944

Supermarine Spitfire Mk VC
5th FS, 52nd FG, Western Desert, 1943

+25-lb/sq in boost pressure for a period not exceeding five minutes. Performance was improved still further at low level, but overhaul life was reduced and 150-octane fuel had to be used in place of the standard 100-octane. Fuel consumption also went up by approximately 25 per cent when the higher boost setting was used in conjunction with maximum revs.

The Mk V featured a revised fuel system, since problems had been experienced with fuel 'boiling' at high altitude. Aircraft were fitted with an immersed electric pump in the bottom tank to assist fuel flow above 25,000 ft and later examples had the separate cock for the top tank omitted. To meet the possibility of engine cutting due to fuel boiling in warm weather at high altitudes, many Spitfire Mk VCs for use in the Middle East had the main tanks pressurised, exhaust air from the aircraft's vacuum pump being admitted to the top tank. As this system impaired the self-sealing qualities of the fuel tanks it had only to be switched on when fuel pressure fell below 6 lb/sq in, or when the fuel pressure warning light illuminated. On occasions, flight at high altitudes in very warm weather could lead to a rich mixture cut with the pressurisation working, in which case the pressure had to be turned off immediately.

Armament configurations were similar to the Spitfire Mk I/Mk II, the Mk VA (of which only 100 were produced) carried eight 0.303-in Browning machine-guns and the Mk VB had two 20-mm Hispano cannon and four Brownings. The Spitfire Mk VC was fitted with the strengthened Type 'C' wing designed to accommodate four 20-mm Hispano cannon – it could also carry a 250-lb bomb under each wing, or a bomb of up to 500 lb in the under-fuselage position. The Mk VB was later used for dive-bombing, but was limited to a single fuselage-mounted bomb. Alternatively, slipper tanks of 30- or 45-Imp gal capacity could be carried to extend range on operations – larger tanks of 90- and 170-Imp gal were cleared for ferrying purposes only. Although some early Spitfire Mk Vs had fabric-covered ailerons, production lines soon switched to metal ailerons as these resulted in a marked improvement in lateral control during high-speed dives. Aircraft already in service were modified as a matter of priority as soon as replacement sets were available. As most Spitfire Mk VCs were

used outside the European theatre of operations, they were fitted with an extended fairing under the nose. This duct contained a filter, together with a shutter that admitted either cold air or hot air warmed by the engine.

The LF.Mk V featured the M-series Merlin and had wing-stiffening strakes on the upper surfaces of the wing over the wheel wells. These were added to strengthen the wings, since the aircraft's role was now confined to operations at low level. The wing tips were easily detached to create the clipped LF, but could be replaced just as easily, and many pilots preferred to retain the Spitfire's classic wing profile. By 1944, the few Spitfire LF.Mk Vs that remained in first-line service were all rather second-hand and were liable to vary greatly as regards their modification state. In an attempt to claw back some of the speed of the original, the carburettor ice-guard was usually removed and some aircraft featured Mk IX multi-ejector exhausts instead of the 'fishtail' type that had been a standard fitment on early Mk Vs. Another improvement was a round streamlined rear-view mirror which largely (but not completely) replaced the oblong 'make-up' mirror used previously. Many older aircraft also retained the externally mounted bulletproof panel on the windscreen, unlike later examples that featured the revised screen which had a much smoother external shape with less drag.

Speed Spitfire

The Speed Spitfire was to have made an attempt on the landplane speed record, but in the event the progressive raising of the record by Germany put it beyond reach. The aircraft chosen to be modified was K9834, which was powered by a sprint version of the Merlin that was ultimately developed to produce 2,122 hp at +27½-lb/sq in boost. The airframe was cleaned up considerably and included flush riveting throughout, an elongated low-drag windscreen, shortened wings, a low-drag pitot tube and a smooth exterior finish. Due to the extra power of the Merlin, the engine bearers and attachment points had to be strengthened and the cooling system was pressurised, and employed an enlarged radiator that necessitated the starboard flap being shortened to allow the radiator to extend all the way to the trailing edge. A four-bladed wooden propeller was fitted, which was of

The Speed Spitfire, N.17, being run-up at Eastleigh. The increased size of the radiator is readily apparent and the oil cooler under the port wing was also of larger diameter. The special sprint Merlin was capable of producing 2,100 hp via a coarse-pitch, four-bladed wooden propeller. (Philip Jarrett)

Right: After the demise of the record attempt, the Speed Spitfire reverted to its original serial number K9834, and was fitted with a Merlin XII with conventional radiator and oil cooler, three-bladed Rotol propeller and standard windscreen, as fitted to PR variants. It was delivered to the PRU in November 1940 and fitted with an oblique F.24 camera. Due to its reduced fuel tankage however, it was not successful for reconnaissance work and was used mainly as a hack.

Below: Another view of the former Speed Spitfire, here looking rather tatty. It was eventually scrapped in 1946. (both Philip Jarrett)

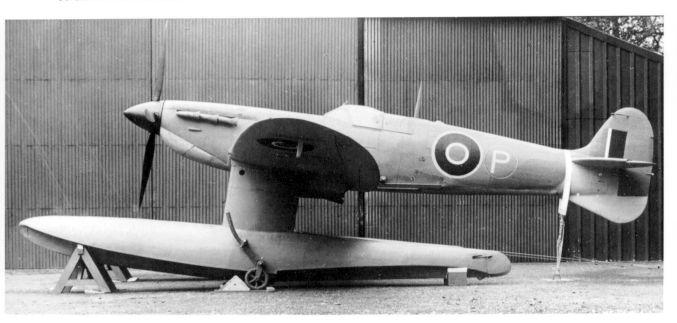

The original-shape tail of the Spitfire floatplane, together with the design of its floats and beaching gear.

EP754 was one of two Spitfire floatplanes converted from Mk Vs by Folland Aircraft. After initial testing at MAEE Helensburgh, W3760, EP751 and EP754 were shipped to the Middle East and flown from the Great Bitter Lake in Egypt in late 1943. No operational use ensued and they were returned to the UK. *(both Philip Jarrett)*

coarse pitch and reduced diameter to avoid drag-rise due to compressibility at maximum revs. Radio equipment was omitted to save weight and a low-drag tailskid was fitted instead of a tailwheel.

The Speed Spitfire, painted in a dark blue and silver scheme and carrying the number N.17, was flown for the first time on 11 November 1938 and early the following year it was ready to be tested. Flight Lieutenant H.A. 'Bruin' Purvis, an RAE test pilot, was selected to fly the aircraft and it eventually achieved a top speed of 408 mph at 3,000 ft. As any record attempt would have to be made at low level (250 ft) this figure would be reduced slightly and it was therefore decided to replace the radiator with a water tank and condenser, to be fitted in the fuselage in place of the upper fuel tank. It was hoped that by reducing drag, speed would be increased, but within a matter of weeks the speed record had been raised beyond the Spitfire's capability, initially by the Heinkel He 100 at 463 mph, and then by the Messerschmitt Me 209 at 469 mph. The revised cooling system was eventually fitted in early 1940, but shortly afterwards the aircraft was converted back to 'standard' condition with a Merlin XII and three-bladed propeller, and delivered to the PRU at Heston. As it still retained reduced fuel capacity due to the removal of the top fuselage tank, its use as a reconnaissance machine was limited and it was mainly used as a high-speed communications aircraft. It was eventually broken up in 1946.

Spitfire Floatplane

Having produced many well known flying-boats and seaplanes, it was, perhaps, fitting that Supermarine should be asked to design a floatplane version of the Spitfire. This was something of a panic measure on the part of the Air Ministry and was brought about by the German invasion of Norway. A Spitfire Mk I (R6722) was allocated for conversion and was fitted with a pair of Blackburn Roc floats for water

The first Spitfire floatplane to fly was W3760, seen here with Jeffrey Quill at the controls and after the fin area had been increased by straightening and extending the leading edge. The filter design has also been altered, to avoid spray thrown up by the floats. (Philip Jarrett)

trials to be conducted by No. 12 Maintenance Unit (MU), Kirkbride. Before airborne trials could be carried out however, British forces were thrown out of Norway and the immediate need for a Spitfire floatplane had passed.

Development was in abeyance for a year, but resurfaced in May 1941 when Supermarine was given a contract for a floatplane version of the Mk III. This progressed as far as the trial of models in Farnborough's water tank, but with the demise of the Mk III, it was clear that any future work would have to revolve around the Spitfire Mk V. When war flared up in the Pacific in December 1941, the prospect of being able to deploy fighters that did not need airfield facilities became attractive once again, and W3760 was fitted with Supermarine-designed floats built by Folland Aircraft. It was flown for the first time by Jeffrey Quill on 12 October 1942 and exhibited excellent handling qualities, both in the air and on the water. In contrast to the supporting struts of the previous design, the floats of W3760 were carried on low-drag cantilever legs and it also featured a four-bladed propeller, a revised rear fuselage with a ventrally mounted fin to aid directional stability, and a tropical filter. Slinging points were added and initially a spin recovery parachute was fitted, together with a guard for the rudder horn balance. Flight trials showed that the ventral fin was not up to the job and so the leading edge of the fin was extended to increase the area of the vertical tail surfaces still further. At the same time a revised filter was fitted, the ducting of which was modified so that it was not affected by spray.

Two more Spitfire Mk Vs were converted as floatplanes by Folland Aircraft (EP751 and EP754) and together with W3760 these were tested at the Marine Aircraft Experimental Establishment (MAEE) at Helensburgh in 1943.

Instead of being sent to the Far East after the trials had been carried out, the floatplanes were dispatched to Egypt, since it was hoped that they could be used to intercept *Luftwaffe* transport aircraft operating in the eastern Mediterranean. The idea came to nothing, however, and the aircraft were returned to the UK in mid-1944 to be Struck off Charge later that year. This was not quite the end of the Spitfire floatplane saga, as a Mark IX (MJ982) was fitted with floats in 1944 (again for possible use in the Pacific) but despite the aircraft being faster than a Hurricane Mk II, once again the idea was dropped.

Seafire Mk I/Mk II/Mk III

Following the successful conversion of two Spitfire Mk VBs (AB205 and AD371) as 'hooked' Spitfires, the first of the type for Naval use was a batch of 48 Mk VBs converted by Air Service Training (AST) at Hamble, in early 1942, as Seafire Mk IBs. As the Fleet Air Arm (FAA) needed these aircraft quickly, no wing folding was incorporated and the only major modification was the fitting of an A-frame arrester hook attached to the bottom longerons at frame 15. The rear fuselage was strengthened to cater for the increased loadings and the frame was faired into the underside of the fuselage to reduce drag. Slinging points were incorporated fore and aft of the cockpit. A further 118 conversions were made by AST, all featuring the 'B' Type wing of the Spitfire Mk VB. The engines fitted to these Seafire Mk IBs ranged between Merlin 45, 46, 50, 50A, 55 and 56, depending on which airframes were selected for conversion.

The next Seafire was the Mk IIC, which had the 'C' Type wing and further fuselage strengthening for the installation of catapult spools and rocket-assisted take-off gear (RATOG). The first aircraft of this variant were fitted with the Merlin 45 or 46, but as these engines were rated for best performance at high altitudes, the Navy found the Seafire's performance at lower levels disappointing. Following a successful trial with a 1,645-hp Merlin 32 in L1004, this engine was selected for the Seafire Mk II, the aircraft's designation being amended to L.Mk IIC. A four-bladed propeller was also fitted and starting was by a Coffman cartridge. In 1943, some aircraft were fitted with two F.24 cameras (one vertical and one oblique) and were classed as LR.Mk IIC machines. Total production of the Seafire Mk II

was 400 (260 by Supermarine and 140 by Westland).

The first Seafire to feature folding wings was the F.Mk III, of which 1,263 were built, 350 by Cunliffe-Owen and 913 by Westland. The wing-folding mechanism was tested on Seafire Mk IIC MA970 and featured two folds, one inboard of the wing cannon and the other at the tip. The first 103 Seafire Mk IIIs were powered by the Merlin 55, all subsequent aircraft being fitted with the 'cropped blower' Merlin 55M for extra performance at low level. These aircraft were designated LF.Mk III. All Seafire Mk IIIs had the capability to use RATOG and could carry either two 250-lb bombs under the wings or a 500-lb bomb under the fuselage. The Mk III was also tested with various weapons loads, including rocket projectiles, smoke floats and mines. The final variant was the FR.Mk III, which was fitted with two F.24 cameras.

During its service life the Seafire took part in most major Naval engagements commencing with the Allied landings in North Africa (Operation *Torch*) on 8 November 1942. The first victory for a Seafire occurred on this day, when a Vichy Dewoitine D.520 was shot down by Sub-Lieutenant G.C. Baldwin, DSC, of No. 807 Squadron, in MA986. Seafires were also active during the invasion of Italy, with eight squadrons providing air support from the escort carriers *Attacker*, *Battler*, *Hunter* and *Stalker*, together with the Fleet carriers *Formidable* and *Illustrious* during the Salerno landings. Immediately after the D-Day landings in Normandy, Seafires flew sorties with the Air Spotting Pool (also known as No. 34 Recce Wing, 2nd Tactical Air Force (TAF)) to direct naval gunfire which was bombarding German fortifications along the French coastline. In February 1944, Seafires of No. 801 Squadron flew from the deck of HMS *Furious* to provide fighter cover for Fairey Barracudas attacking German convoys along the Norwegian coast, and later in the year were involved in attacks on the German battleship *Tirpitz*. By 1945 Seafires were operational in the Far East, providing cover for the invasion of Rangoon and Penang, and escort for raids on Japanese oil refineries in Sumatra. At the time of the Japanese surrender eight squadrons were still equipped with the Seafire Mk III, although these were quickly phased out and replaced by the Griffon-engined Seafire Mk XV.

Appendix 1. Specifications and Performance

Spitfire Mk IA
Dimensions: length 29 ft 11 in; height 11 ft 5 in; span 36 ft 10 in; wing area 242 sq ft
Powerplant: one Rolls-Royce Merlin II or III of 1,030 hp
Weights: empty 4,341 lb; loaded 5,800 lb
Armament: Eight 0.303-in Browning machine-guns (300 rounds per gun)
Gunsight: GM.2 reflector
Radio: TR.9B
Performance: maximum speed 364 mph at 19,000 ft; initial rate of climb 2,530 ft per minute; service ceiling 31,500 ft; normal range 395 miles

Spitfire LF.Mk VB (clipped wings)
Dimensions: length 29 ft 11 in; height 11 ft 5½ in; span 32 ft 2 in; wing area 231 sq ft
Powerplant: one Rolls-Royce Merlin 45M/50M/ 55M of 1,440 hp
Weights: empty 5,050 lb; loaded 6,650 lb
Armament: two 20-mm Hispano cannon (60 rounds per gun), plus four 0.303-in Browning machine-guns (350 rounds per gun)
Gunsight: GM.2 reflector
Radio: TR 1133, TR 1143, ARI 5000, or TR.9D
Performance: maximum speed 357 mph at 6,000 ft; initial rate of climb 4,750 ft per minute; service ceiling 35,500 ft; normal range 470 miles

Appendix 2. Weapons and Stores

In contrast with some other fighters of the period, the Spitfire's armament did not show any great variety and was standardised around the 0.303-in Browning machine-gun and 20-mm Hispano cannon. In the mid- to late-war period, the Spitfire Mk V gave sterling service in the ground-attack role carrying a bomb of up to 500 lb under the fuselage or two 250-lb bombs under the wings (Mk VC).

Spitfire Mk I X4257 had a long history and was the first production aircraft to carry two 20-mm Hispano cannon in the 'B' wing. It was first flown on 17 August 1940 and converted to Mk VB standard in February 1941. Following service with Nos 92, 411 and 242 Squadrons, X4257 was modified as an LF.Mk VB and flew with No. 118 Squadron, before being taken on by No. 64 Squadron, with which it was coded 'SH-C'. It was written off in a forced landing on 3 July 1944 that killed its pilot, Flying Officer Wally Smart. *(Philip Jarrett)*

Browning 0.303-in machine-gun

Designed before World War One as an infantry weapon, the Browning machine-gun was produced by the Colt company of America and was belt-fed and recoil-operated. It was first tested by the RAF in a Bristol Fighter in July 1918. Such was the leisurely pace of development in the inter-war years, the next use of the gun was in an Armstrong Whitworth Siskin in June 1931. The Siskin trials were a complete success, but by this time Colt had completely redesigned the gun for use in aircraft and the revised weapon was known as the '1930 pattern'. Examples of the new Browning were demonstrated at Vickers-Armstrong and all further trials were with the revised model. In June 1934, the Browning was chosen to replace the 0.303-in Vickers Mk III, its advantages including an increased rate of fire from 800 to 1,100 rounds per minute, improved reliability and a reduction in weight.

Further trials at A&AEE Martlesham Heath brought evidence of a potential problem, when a gun 'cooked off' after firing a 100-round burst.

Like all recoil-operated guns, when the Browning stopped firing, a round remained in the chamber and the firing pin was cocked. After the burst, the barrel had become so hot that it heated up the cartridge, which detonated the cordite propellant. Other less volatile propellants could not be used as the RAF was tied to Army stocks of ammunition and so the gun had to be modified so that the breech block was held at the rear of the gun with the chamber empty. Difficulty was also experienced with the feed mechanism, the redesign to overcome this particular snag resulting in the British gun being very different from the original.

Other problems occurred when the gun was in service – the most serious defect being known as a 'separated case' stoppage. It was possible to adjust the position of the barrel relative to the breech block and if the barrel of the gun was too far forward, too much of the cartridge case protruded from the barrel and the end was blown off. Before armourers had gained the necessary experience, stoppages were a regular occurrence. The final major modification to the gun involved a revision of the muzzle attachment to allow longer bursts to be fired without the risk of fouling, which was liable to result in a seized barrel. By the time of the Battle of Britain, the Browning was an extremely reliable gun, but the effectiveness of even an eight-gun battery was soon questioned as Luftwaffe bombers were well protected in terms of armour and self-sealing fuel tanks. The answer lay in the explosive 20-mm shell.

Hispano 20-mm cannon

This weapon first appeared as the 'Hispano Moteur Cannon' in the mid-1930s and was designed to be an integral part of the Hispano V-12 engine. It utilised a round of 4.4 oz and was capable of firing 700 rounds per minute. With a muzzle velocity of 2,820 ft per second, its penetrative power was 50 per cent greater than that of the Russian ShVak, and double the power of the German Oerlikon. Following trials with a Hispano-armed Dewoitine D.510 at A&AEE in 1937, the gun was adopted by the Air Ministry, even though its development was far from complete. It was initially intended for the Hawker Tornado/Typhoon, but following the Munich crisis in 1938, it was decided to equip the Spitfire and Hurricane with the Hispano as soon as possible.

A Spitfire Mk VC of No. 2 (SAAF) Squadron carries a 250-lb bomb in the under-fuselage position. With its strengthened wing, the Mk VC could also carry two 250-lb bombs under the wings. *(Philip Jarrett)*

Following trial use of the cannon-armed Mk I L1007 by various squadrons in early 1940, the first definitive Spitfire Mk IBs appeared in the summer of 1940 for use by No. 19 Squadron at Duxford. Although the weapon had a devastating effect, its reliability was so poor that it was quickly withdrawn. The Hispano weighed 109 lb and was never meant to be fitted in the relatively flimsy structure of an aircraft wing. These installation problems were compounded by the 60-round magazine, which dictated that the gun be mounted on its side to avoid an overly large bulge on the wing's upper surface. This led to several complications, including difficulty in getting the empty cartridge cases to eject cleanly. A potentially dangerous condition known as a 'lightly struck cap stoppage' was also experienced. This could be due to a weak breech block return spring, or a situation where the cartridge was 'crushed up' excessively in the chamber, either eventuality resulting in the firing pin having insufficient impact to fire the round. With an unfired round in the chamber, the release of the next round could cause an explosion within the gun body. This was highly dangerous not only for the unfortunate pilot, but also for his wingman, who was likely to be confronted with a wing panel and other debris heading rapidly in his direction. The use of a triple wire return spring and a slight shortening of the chamber (together with a longer firing pin) largely overcame these problems.

Difficulties with the 60-round magazine led to the development of a belt-feed mechanism that

Right: Spitfire Mk VC BR202 testing the 170-Imp gal slipper tank in flight. This machine was modified by Boulton Paul and featured a deeper nose profile for an enlarged oil tank. Eighteen flights were made from Gibraltar to Malta before the end of 1942, by which time this method of reinforcement was no longer necessary.

Spitfire Mk VB (trop) AB320, fitted with a 90-Imp gal slipper tank. *(both Philip Jarrett)*

was first used in 1941. Reliability was much improved but another problem arose as the belt-feed was operated by the gun's recoil, and its movement relative to the mounting was sometimes insufficient to operate the feed, which led to a stoppage. This tended to vary between individual aircraft, and armourers had to resort to adjusting the recoil unit for each gun separately. Eventually the Hispano became an extremely reliable and effective weapon but it did take time for armourers to come to terms with its idiosyncrasies, and in the meantime pilots' combat reports would frequently complain of a stoppage. If this happened the recoil from the working gun would tend to slew the aircraft in yaw and make aiming impossible. In such a situation a pilot could, if necessary, revert to using machine-guns only by pressing the top indent of the firing strip mounted on the control column.

External fuel tanks

The first external tank to be used operationally on the Spitfire was a 30-Imp gal blister tank mounted under the port wing of the PR.Mk IC, as used by the Photographic Development Unit in 1940. A similar blister under the starboard wing, but with a flat undersurface, contained two F.24 cameras. The PR.Mk IF had its cameras mounted in the rear fuselage so that blister tanks could be fitted under both wings. Following experiments with fixed tanks on the Spitfire Mk I in 1940, 100 Spitfire Mk IIAs were modified to LR standard in mid-1941 with a 40-Imp gal tank mounted under the port wing. This was to allow them to provide escort for Handley Page Hampden bombers attacking the *Scharnhorst* and *Gneisenau* in Brest harbour, but the asymmetric installation caused adverse handling characteristics, as Sergeant Walter Johnston of No. 152 Squadron recalls: 'When we got the awful long-range Spitfires we all had very narrow escapes. Take-off was full right rudder and stick almost hard over in the same direction. This was due to the extra weight on the port wing only. Flying circuits and bumps to get the feel was dicey as it meant take-offs and landings with a full wing tank. There was no such thing as a typical curving Spitfire approach to keep the ground in sight – not with about 250–300 lb on the inner wing. So we trundled in as if the runway was that of a carrier. Some of us did forget and had hair-raising things happen. We lost two pilots who just undercooked the turn and slipped in.'

Streamlined slipper tanks mounted under the centre section were more successful – there were no undesirable handling problems, although top speed was reduced by 20–30 mph. Unlike the fixed installation of the long-range Spitfire Mk IIAs,

these tanks were designed to be jettisoned before entering combat (any malfunction with the jet (jettisonable) tank normally meant an abort) and were of 30- or 45-Imp gal capacity. Oversize tanks of 90 and 170 Imp gal were used to ferry Spitfire Mk Vs to Malta in 1942, the latter allowing a direct flight from Gibraltar, which meant that the services of an aircraft-carrier were not required. Some aircraft were modified locally to carry a 45-Imp gal cylindrical tank, more commonly seen on Mk IXs, instead of the normal slipper type.

Appendix 3. Production Details

Of all the design considerations that R.J. Mitchell took into account when formulating the Spitfire, the need for mass production was not one of them. If it had been, the Spitfire would probably have emerged in a rather different form, one that was rather more conducive to ease of manufacture than outright aerodynamic efficiency. Whereas the structure of the Hurricane owed much to the long line of classic Hawker fighters that preceded it, the Spitfire embraced the new technology of stressed skin construction with no concessions to anything but performance. Mitchell's philosophy contrasted with that of Willi Messerschmitt, who achieved a similar goal with the Bf 109, but with a machine that had the principles of production engineering designed into it from the very beginning, so that it took only around one-third of the man-hours to build. Due to the complexities of the Spitfire airframe, especially the very thin elliptical wing, production in the period 1937-39 suffered serious delays and cost overruns.

Initially, Spitfire production was centred on the Woolston Works in Southampton with assembly

and flight testing taking place at the nearby airfield at Eastleigh. In 1939 a new factory was opened on the River Itchen but as at Woolston, only fuselages were produced, the wings being sub-contracted to General Aircraft at Feltham and Pobjoy Airmotors. As production Spitfires were vastly different from the prototype, a long list of requirements as laid out in Specification F.16/36 had to be incorporated, one of the major items being a stiffening of the wings to ensure freedom from flutter up to a never-exceed speed (Vne) of 470 mph IAS. As Supermarine's staff numbered only around 500 when the first contract for 310 Spitfires was received in June 1936, a severe strain was put on the company, since not only had it to gear up for large-scale production, it also had to completely revise all drawings in response to the Air Ministry's demands. As delivery targets slipped further behind schedule, accusations began to fly, with Supermarine blaming the sub-contractors for late delivery of components and the sub-contractors blaming Supermarine for late delivery of the relevant drawings.

Recently located by Philip Jarrett, this photograph shows the legendary Eastleigh coat-racks suspended above Spitfire Mk I K9841. Workers' outdoor clothes were hung up and then hoisted well out of reach, an excellent way of beating anyone who was prone to sneaking off home early. K9841 flew with Nos 66, 611, 609 and 616 Squadrons, before moving to No. 72 Squadron on 2 September 1940. Eight days later it was written off in a forced landing after suffering combat damage. Pilot Officer E.E. Males was uninjured, but was shot down and killed on 27 September in X4340. *(Philip Jarrett)*

The first production Spitfire should have been rolled out in October 1937 but did not take to the air until 14 May 1938, since Supermarine-built fuselages had been gathering dust at Woolston waiting for wings to arrive. Over the next few months production gradually gathered pace – by the end of 1938, some 49 Spitfires had been delivered to the RAF and by June 1940 this figure had risen to 800. By this time steps had been taken to increase production capacity

significantly with the setting up of the factory at Castle Bromwich near Birmingham. The first of 11,939 Spitfires built at the plant (Mk IIA P7280), was delivered on 27 June 1940 and production would ultimately peak at 320 a week in the summer of 1944. The Castle Bromwich works had initially been run by Morris Motors, since it was thought that Lord Nuffield's organisation would be able to mass produce Spitfires just as it had mass produced cars. Unfortunately, the

Spitfire Mk I P9516 first took to the air on 25 April 1940 and flew in the Battle of Britain with No. 65 Squadron. It is shown here being repaired following a forced landing with No. 222 Squadron on 14 January 1941, in which it turned over. P9516 subsequently served with No. 132 Squadron at Peterhead and was destroyed when it flew into the ground on 29 November 1941. *(Philip Jarrett)*

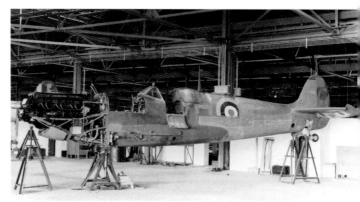

RAF's constant demand for modifications and improvements led to the whole process breaking down with no finished aircraft appearing at the end of the line. Nuffield was relieved of his authority and the factory placed under the control of Vickers, which revised working practices accordingly, to avoid the bottlenecks that had brought production to a halt.

In Southampton a limited dispersal of production had taken place before the devastating raids that hit the main factories at

Spitfire repairs being carried out by Rolls-Royce at Hucknall in the early stages of World War Two. *(Philip Jarrett)*

the height of the Battle of Britain. The most serious disruption was caused by an attack on 26 September 1940, which damaged the Woolston and Itchen works to such an extent that it was decided to end production and set up dispersed facilities at other sites away from the south coast. Production was started in Salisbury, Reading and Trowbridge, with final assembly taking place at High Post, Henley and Keevil

A Spitfire Mk VC having its Merlin engine fitted. The carefully shaped oil tank under the engine bearers is clearly evident. (Philip Jarrett)

airfields, respectively. By July 1941, a second airfield had been formed to serve the Salisbury production line at Chattis Hill. Sub-assembly manufacture was divided among many local businesses, with garages being by far the most numerous. Other facilities requisitioned included rolling mills, laundries, bus stations and various factory buildings.

Despite the loss of the main works at Woolston and Itchen, deliveries were not seriously affected, thanks mainly to Castle Bromwich and the prior transfer of production to smaller engineering works within Southampton, a scheme masterminded by Leonard Gooch and Gilbert Olsen, the latter being among the ninety dead when a bomb hit an air raid shelter during an attack on Woolston on 24 September 1940. Following the attacks, Hursley Park near Winchester was taken over to provide a secure location for the design and administrative staff and a hangar was erected in the grounds for experimental production.

In addition to the manufacture of Spitfires in and around Southampton and at Castle Bromwich, Westland Aircraft at Yeovil began production in August 1940, with an order for 300 Spitfire Mk IAs (subsequently amended to include 140 Mk VBs and 110 Mk VCs). Further contracts were awarded for 200 and 185 Spitfire Mk Vs, and from mid-1942 Westland became prime contractor for Merlin-engined Seafires, initially with a contract to convert 213 Spitfire Mk VBs to Seafire Mk IIC standard, followed by the production of 913 Seafire Mk IIIs. Westland was also responsible for the production of 350 Seafire Mk IIIs by Cunliffe-Owen under sub-contract.

Repair units

Repair units situated throughout the country played an important role in maintaining the flow of aircraft to the RAF, since large numbers of damaged aircraft were returned in 'as new' condition. One such unit was run by the London, Midland and Scottish Railway (LMS) and was situated at Barassie on the Ayrshire coast. LMS possessed a huge engineering organisation with a workforce of almost 30,000, many of whom had been given over to the production of aircraft components and tanks. In addition to this work, the larger workshops took on the task of repairing Hampden, Armstrong Whitworth Whitley and Avro Lancaster bombers, while the former paint shop at Barassie was converted so that it could carry out Spitfire repairs.

While selected staff were away at Derby for training on aircraft repair, an airstrip was laid down next to the works and the first Spitfire to be repaired at Barassie was completed on 10 October 1941 and flown from the adjacent runway to Prestwick for flight testing. Initially the work was carried out as a sub-contract for Scottish Aviation Ltd, but from March 1942

LMS carried out the work on a direct contract. Planning had allowed for a maximum number of 12 aircraft to be present in the works at any one time, but this was soon exceeded, and by August 1942 some 26 Spitfires were being worked on. At this time production and inspection staff numbered 510. To ease congestion, two 'Super-Robin' hangars were erected which enabled up to 25 fuselages and mainplanes to be dealt with in the original shop, with a maximum of ten aircraft in the hangars for final assembly. By the end of March 1944, 94 Spitfires had been returned to the air.

Total production for the Spitfire Mk I amounted to 1,583 and there were 920 Spitfire Mk IIs. Of these 750 were produced as Mk IIAs and 170 as Mk IIBs. Of all Spitfire variants, the Mk V was the most prolific, a total of 6,479 being built, but of these only 100 were machine-gun armed Spitfire Mk VAs, all the rest being cannon-armed Spitfire Mk VBs and Spitfire Mk VCs.

Appendix 4. Museum Aircraft and Warbirds

In marked contrast to many other classic warbirds, the world's Spitfire population is reasonably healthy and, in addition to static examples, around 50 aircraft (all marks) are currently airworthy, or potentially airworthy. The following information gives details of some of the more notable early-mark Spitfires.

K9942 (Mk IA)
Built by Supermarine, K9942 was first flown on 21 April 1939 by George Pickering and was delivered to No. 72 Squadron at Church Fenton. It was subsequently used by No. 7 OTU (re-numbered No. 57 OTU in December 1940) and, following a flying accident in February 1942, by No. 53 OTU. It was acquired by the Admiralty in March 1944, but was then earmarked for preservation, and is a popular exhibit at the RAF Museum at Hendon.

P7350 (Mk IIA)
Currently resident with the Battle of Britain Memorial Flight (BBMF) at Coningsby, P7350 was built at Castle Bromwich in 1940 and first went to No. 266 Squadron as 'UO-T' before moving to No. 603 Squadron. It later flew with

Nos 616 and 64 Squadrons, before spending ten months with the Central Gunnery School (CGS) from April 1942 to February 1943. P7350 was sold for scrap in 1944, but was presented to RAF Colerne for display. It remained there until 1967, when it was restored to flying condition for the Battle of Britain film. P7350 moved to the BBMF in 1968.

P7973 (Mk IIA)
Built at Castle Bromwich, P7973 was issued to No. 222 Squadron in April 1941, but within a month had transferred to No. 452 (RAAF) Squadron where, among others, it was flown by Squadron Leader K.W. 'Bluey' Truscott. By August 1941 it was with No. 313 Squadron, but suffered a flying accident in February 1942 and, after repair, was passed to No. 57 OTU. It later flew with No. 61 OTU and the CGS before being presented to Australia, where it was put on display at the Australian War Memorial Museum in Canberra.

P8332 (Mk IIB)
P8332 was built at Castle Bromwich and joined No. 222 Squadron on 21 April 1942, coded 'ZD-L'. It also carried the presentation title *Soebang* following the donation of funds from the Netherlands East Indies. It was damaged on 23 August 1941 and the following April was transferred to Canada, where it was taken on

One Spitfire that did not make it into long-term preservation, Mk II G-AHZI *Josephine* was former P8727, which flew with No. 276 Squadron as an ASR.Mk IIC (Merlin 45). It is seen here with L.V. Worsdell (Chief Pilot at Marshalls of Cambridge) in the cockpit. This machine was written off in a take-off crash at Kastrup, Copenhagen on 15 April 1947. *(Philip Jarrett)*

strength by No. 1 Training Command, Mountain View, Ontario. It is presently on display at the Museum of Science and Technology in Ottawa.

P9444 (Mk IA)
Supermarine-built and first flown on 2 April 1940, P9444 was used for trials at Farnborough before joining No. 72 Squadron. It was damaged on 3 July 1940 and after work by No. 1 Civilian Repair Unit flew with Nos 58, 61 and 53 OTUs. It is currently on display at the Science Museum in London.

R6915 (Mk IA)
The Imperial War Museum's R6915 is a veteran of the Battle of Britain, having flown with No. 609 Squadron. Built by Supermarine, it was delivered to No. 609 Squadron on 21 July 1940 and was taken on its first sortie by Pilot Officer Noel Agazarian. Over the next four months it flew 58 sorties and was credited with three aircraft destroyed, plus two shared, two probables and four damaged. Agazarian claimed three kills (1½ x Bf 110, 1 x Bf 109, ½ x He 111) with Flying Officer J.C. Dundas (elder brother of Hugh) claiming one Bf 109 while flying the aircraft. Following service with No. 602 Squadron in 1941, R6915 flew with Nos 61 and 57 OTUs before being Struck off Charge in 1947.

P9306 (Mk IA)
Another survivor of the Battle of Britain, P9306 flew with No. 74 Squadron and was used by Pilot Officer P.C.F. Stevenson to shoot down a Bf 109E on 6 July, although this was not confirmed. P9306 also flew with No. 131 Squadron and Nos 52 and 61 OTUs before being donated to the USA in 1944. It remains on display at the Museum of Science and Industry in Chicago.

X4590 (Mk IA)
Built by Supermarine, X4590 was flown for the first time on 30 September 1940 by George Pickering and was then delivered to No. 609 Squadron. It was damaged on 25 October, but re-appeared with No. 66 Squadron on 24 February 1941 after repair. It also served with No. 57 OTU and No. 303 Squadron, before being allocated for preservation in August 1944. It is currently on show in the Battle of Britain Hall at the RAF Museum, Hendon.

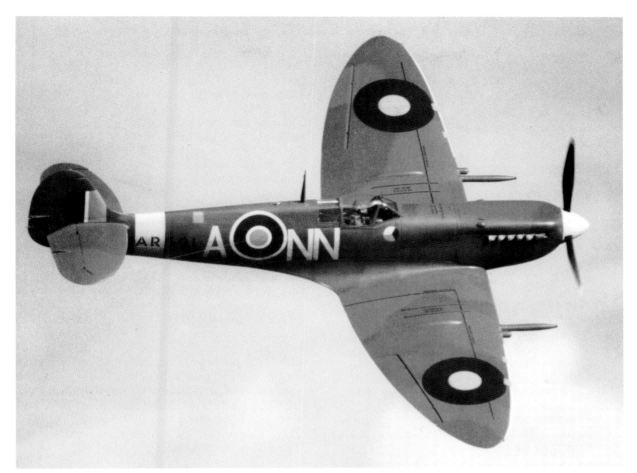

The Shuttleworth Collection's well known Spitfire LF.Mk VC AR501, in the colours of No. 310 (Czech) Squadron. At the time of its arrival at Shuttleworth, the total flying time for AR501 amounted to 511 hours 35 minutes. *(Philip Jarrett)*

AB910 (LF.Mk VB)

Perhaps the best known of all airworthy Spitfire Mk Vs, AB910 was built at Castle Bromwich in 1941 and was initially allocated to No. 222 Squadron. After a brief spell with No. 130 Squadron, AB910 was used by No. 133 (Eagle) Squadron, with which it was flown on two occasions by Pilot Officer Don Gentile. Prior to service with No. 53 OTU, it was flown by Nos 242, 416 and 402 Squadrons. Its final service use was with No. 527 Squadron, which became the Radio Warfare Establishment. AB910 was bought by Allen Wheeler in 1947 as G-AISU and in 1959 it was sold to Vickers-Armstrong Ltd. In 1965 the company donated it to the BBMF, with which it still flies.

AR213 (Mk IA)

Built by Westland, AR213 flew with No. 57 OTU (coded 'JZ-E') and No. 53 OTU before being Struck off Charge in November 1945. Purchased by Allen Wheeler in March 1947, it was registered G-AIST but was stored until refurbished for the Battle of Britain film in 1967. Sold to The Hon. Patrick Lindsay in 1978, AR213 continued to be used by its owner until Lindsay's death in 1986, whereupon it was sold to Victor Gauntlet. It is currently based at Booker.

AR501 (LF.Mk VC)

AR501 was built by Westland and delivered in July 1942 to No. 310 Squadron at Exeter, where it was flown on several occasions by Battle of Britain ace Squadron Leader Frantisek Dolezal, DFC. In March 1943 AR501 (coded 'NN-A') was damaged when hit by a de Havilland Mosquito which swung on take-off. After repair the Spitfire passed through No. 33 MU, No. 3501 SU, and No. 504 Squadron, before serving with another Czech squadron, No. 312. Before being Struck off Charge, AR501 flew with No. 442 Squadron, No. 58 OTU, No. 1 TEU, No. 61 OTU and the CGS. In 1946 it was delivered to the Department of Aeronautical Engineering at Loughborough College, where it remained until moved to the Shuttleworth Collection in 1961. After more than 40 years it is still based at Old Warden.

AR614 (Mk VC)

Also built by Westland, AR614 was first issued to No. 312 Squadron at Harrowbeer in September 1942. Coded 'DU-Z', it was flown by Squadron Leader Tomas Vybiral on 14 May 1943 when it suffered flak damage during a strafing attack on St Peter Port, Guernsey. After repairs, AR614 passed briefly through Nos 610, 130 and 222 Squadrons before arriving at No. 53 OTU, where it remained until June 1945. By 1963 AR614 was on the dump at Dishforth, but was sold to Canada, where it was registered C-FDUY. By 1993 it was back in the UK as G-BUWA and was rebuilt by Historic Flying for Sir Tim Wallis's Alpine Fighter Collection. In 1999 AR614 was sold to Paul Allen's Seattle-based Flying Heritage Collection.

BL370 (Mk VB)

BL370 was delivered to No. 130 Squadron on 8 December 1941 and subsequently served with Nos 224, 610, 350 and 118 Squadrons, before joining No. 64 Squadron on 19 September 1943, where it was coded 'SH-J'. On 11 August 1944 it passed to No. 53 OTU, but crashed near the Humber Estuary on 30 September. The remains were partially rebuilt by Steve Arnold and Julian Mitchell, but were sold in November 1996 to Patrick F. Taylor who has since completed the restoration. It is now displayed at the US National D-Day Museum in New Orleans.

BL614 (Mk VB)

BL614 was built at Castle Bromwich in December 1941 and joined No. 611 Squadron at Drem two months later. It was taken over by No. 242 Squadron and in turn was passed to No. 222 Squadron, before moving to Ayr, where it was taken on charge by No. 64 Squadron in March 1943. By the summer it was based at West Malling and took part in a number of bomber escorts in connection with Operation *Starkey*, a large-scale invasion deception that took place in September 1943. Further service in Scotland followed. After the war BL614 became an instructional airframe and was used statically in the Battle of Britain film. In 1982 it was put on show at the Manchester Air and Space Museum and in 1995 went to Rochester for restoration by the Medway Aircraft Preservation Society. It is now on display at the RAF Museum at Hendon.

BL628 (LF.Mk VB)

Ex-Castle Bromwich, BL628 was issued to No. 401 Squadron in April 1942 as 'YO-D'. Later in the year it passed through Nos 308, 167 and 610 Squadrons, before suffering an accident in November 1942. After repair it was allocated to the Admiralty and converted as a 'hooked' Spitfire for use by No. 719 Squadron at St Merryn. It is currently owned in Australia by Peter Croser and registered as VH-FVB.

BM597 (Mk VB)

Also built at Castle Bromwich, BM597 had a short operational career with No. 315 Squadron at Woodvale and later flew with No. 317 Squadron as 'JH-C'. After suffering Category B damage in February 1943, it underwent a lengthy period of storage before being delivered to No. 58 OTU. Gate guardian duties followed at Hednesford and Bridgnorth, and after involvement with the Battle of Britain film, BM597 was put on the gate at Linton-on-Ouse and then Church Fenton. It was eventually restored by Historic Flying, and is now operated by the Historic Aircraft Collection and based at Duxford.

EE853 (Mk VC)

EE853 was built by Westland and shipped to Australia in March 1943, where it became 'UP-O' of No. 79 Squadron. It saw service in New Guinea, but was written off on landing at Kiriwana on 28 August 1943 and abandoned. Rediscovered in 1971 by Langdon Badger, EE853 has been progressively restored and is currently with the South Australia Aviation Museum at Port Adelaide.

EP120 (Mk VB)

Built at Castle Bromwich in early 1942, EP120 first flew with No. 501 Squadron, initially as 'SD-L', but later as 'SD-Y'. It subsequently flew with No. 19 Squadron, before being delivered to No. 402 Squadron at Digby, where it was coded 'AE-A' and flown on a number of occasions by Squadron Leader Lloyd Chadburn. Following Chadburn's promotion to Wing Leader in June 1943, EP120 was flown by Squadron Leader Geoff Northcott, who shot down four Bf 109s

and two Fw 190s in the aircraft between 27 June and 3 November 1943. Following short stays at No. 33 MU and No. 3501 SU, EP120 went to No. 53 OTU and after the war was used as an instructional airframe. Gate guardian duties at Wattisham lasted until 1989, when it was brought indoors and rebuilt to airworthy condition by Historic Flying. It is currently owned by The Fighter Collection and based at Duxford.

Other surviving Spitfire Mk Vs

These include:

BR108: At the National War Museum, Valletta, Malta. Ex-Nos 249 and 603 Squadrons.
BR545: RAAF Museum, Point Cook, Australia.
JK448: Yugoslav Aeronautical Museum, Belgrade.
MA863: USAF Museum, Dayton, Ohio.

Appendix 5. Model Kits

Airfix

Aircraft	Scale	Reference no.	Remarks
Spitfire Mk I	1:72	1071	Decals for 'AZ-H' No. 234 Squadron, P3277, Middle Wallop, August 1940
Spitfire Mk V	1:72	2046	Decals for No. 303 (Polish) Squadron, or 31st Fighter Group, USAAF
Spitfire Mk I	1:24	12001	Decals for 'KL-B' of No. 54 Squadron (Flt Lt Al Deere) Hornchurch, 1940, or 'LO-B' of No. 602 'City of Glasgow' Squadron, Drem, 1939
Spitfire Mk VC trop	1:48	4100	Decals for No. 92 Squadron, North Africa, Nov 42–Feb 43, or Mk VB of No. 457 Squadron, Jurby, Isle of Man, Dec 41–March 42
Spitfire Mk VC/ Seafire Mk IIIC	1:48	5110	Decals for Spitfire Mk VC of No. 79 Squadron RAAF, or Mk VC of No. 2 Squadron/No. 7 Wing SAAF, or Mk VC of No. 103 MU, or Seafire Mk IIIC

Hasegawa

Aircraft	Scale	Reference no.	Remarks
Spitfire Mk VB	1:48	9104	Decals for 'YO-Q' of No. 401 Squadron
Spitfire Mk VB	1:48	9315	Decals for 'JU-H' of No. 111 Squadron – 'nightfighter' matt black
Spitfire Mk VB	1:48	9405	Decals for 'T-L' of No. 249 Squadron, Malta

Italeri

Aircraft	Scale	Reference no.	Remarks
Spitfire Mk VC	1:72	001	Decals for 'T-L' of No. 249 Squadron, Malta

ProModeler

Aircraft	Scale	Reference no.	Remarks
Spitfire Mk VB	1:48	5941	Decals for No. 315 Squadron, Northolt, or No. 402 Squadron, or the 67th Reconnaissance Group, USAAF

Revell

Aircraft	Scale	Reference no.	Remarks
Spitfire Mk II	1:32	4715	Decals for P7840 'GW-Z' of No. 340 Squadron, Ayr, April 1942
Spitfire LF.Mk VB	1:72	4152	Combat set with Bf 109G-10

Revell/Monogram

Aircraft	Scale	Reference no.	Remarks
Spitfire Mk II	1:48	5239	Decals for 'NK-K' of No. 118 Squadron, Ibsley
Spitfire Mk I	1:32	5516	Decals for 'PR-Z' of No. 609 Squadron

SMER

Aircraft	Scale	Reference no.	Remarks
Spitfire Mk VB	1:72	0847	Decals for 'RY-S' of No. 313 Squadron
Spitfire Mk VC	1:72	0871	Decals for 'ZP-X' of No. 457 (RAAF) Squadron
Spitfire Mk VB	1:72	0887	Decals for 'DU-K' of No. 312 Squadron

Tamiya

Aircraft	Scale	Reference no.	Remarks
Spitfire Mk I	1:72	60748	Decals for 'DW-O' of No. 610 Squadron, Biggin Hill
Spitfire Mk VB	1:72	60756	Decals for EN821 'SN-M' of No. 243 Squadron, Ouston, June 1942
Spitfire Mk I	1:48	61032	Decals for aircraft of No. 92 or 610 Squadrons
Spitfire Mk VB	1:48	61033	Decals for aircraft of Nos 243 or 316 Squadrons, or personal machine of Wg Cdr A.G. 'Sailor' Malan
Spitfire Mk VC trop	1:48	61035	Decals for 'AN-V' of No. 417 Squadron, North Africa

Appendix 6. Further Reading

Spitfire – The Canadians by Robert Bracken, Stoddart Publishing, 1995

The Darlington Spitfire by Peter Caygill, Airlife Publishing Ltd, 1999

Spitfire Mark V In Action by Peter Caygill, Airlife Publishing Ltd, 2001

Spitfires Over Sicily by Brian Cull with Malizia and Galea, Grub Street, 2000

Spitfire – Flying Legend by John Dibbs and Tony Holmes, Osprey, 1996

Spitfire, RAF Fighter by AVM Ron Dick, Airlife Publishing Ltd

Buck McNair – Canadian Spitfire Ace by Norman Franks, Grub Street, 2001

Sigh For A Merlin – Testing The Spitfire by Alex Henshaw, Crecy, 1999

Spitfire – The Combat History by Robert Jackson, Airlife Publishing Ltd

Spitfire – The History by Eric B. Morgan and Edward Shacklady, Key Publishing, 1987

Spitfires and Polished Metal by Graham Moss and Barry McKee, Airlife, 1999

The Spitfire Story by Alfred Price, Arms and Armour Press, 1986

Spitfire – A Documentary History by Alfred Price, Macdonald and Jane's, 1977

Spitfire At War by Alfred Price, Ian Allan, 1974

Spitfire At War – 2 by Alfred Price, Ian Allan, 1985

Spitfire Mark I/II Aces 1939–41 by Alfred Price, Osprey, 1996

Spitfire Mark V Aces 1941–45 by Alfred Price, Osprey, 1997

Spitfire – A Test Pilot's Story by Jeffrey Quill, Crecy, 1998

Kiwi Spitfire Ace by Jack Rae, Grub Street, 2001

Spitfire – The Story of a Famous Fighter by Bruce Robertson, Harleyford

Bader's Tangmere Spitfires – The Untold Story 1941 by Dilip Sarkar, Patrick Stevens Ltd, 1996

Spitfire In Action by Jerry Scutts, Squadron/Signal, 1980

Malta – The Spitfire Year 1942 by Christopher Shores and Brian Cull, with Nicola Malizia, Grub Street, 1991

Hornchurch Offensive Vols 1 and 2 by Richard C. Smith, Grub Street

Index